DOWN 2 EARTH

My INTUITIVE WORLD

by
Annie Conboy
Intuitive Medium & Psychic

First Printing 2017
Down 2 Earth Products
Suite 4 Burlees House
Hangingroyd Lane
Hebden Bridge
HX7 7DD
ISBN 978-0-244-32810-8

For my beautiful Desert Rogue. You reshaped my life.
I love you for helping me write again.

Dear Ian, shine your light out into
the world. You are here to bring
in the love vibration and love
will always surround you.
      Love & Light
        Annie Cowboy xxx

Copy No: 5

CONTENTS

Acknowledgements

My journey has been filled with prompts, support and love from many special people. I know I have been really blessed. This book would have been very different without all of the help I have received over many years. A list of all the people who have gifted me their time, energy, attention and love would fill many pages. However, I want to try to mention some of them. If your name isn't on this shorter list please accept my apology. Everyone who contributes to my intuitive world has co-authored this book with me and is sent my gratitude.

The most important person in my life, and the one who opened the intuitive door for me, is my daughter. She has challenged me to find out why. In that search magical events have happened. And my views about the meaning of life have altered radically. I take my inspiration from the wish to bring about a better world for her, her peers and all of the children to come afterwards.

The lady who started me on my journey, Margaret, is a beautiful Light in the Spirit World. Along with my compassionate friend Christine, a gifted yet private medium, both of them opened my mind to the unexplained. Their natural joy in discovery through experience fuelled my interest in many things I had previously dismissed. They got me doing rather than pooh-phooing.

I would like to thank Paul Hunt and all of the people who were involved with Colne Spiritualist church. Paul ran a lovely development circle where the Spirit World finally got their chance to get me working. He is also the medium who got me standing in front of people giving public messages.

Here I must also mention all of the students who have come to me for their own development. They have taught me so much too. I especially want to mention Maura, Helen, John, Simon, Claire, Irene, Jackie, Wendy and Helinka who put up with my insistence on evidence, laughed with me through the paranormal nights and allowed me to explore my own ability to work in altered states of consciousness. The gift of your energy has had an immense impact on my own abilities.

Several people have expanded my work for Spirit by pointing me at new experiences. Thank you to Louise for the idea of Reiki, to Pat for bringing my artwork alive, to David and the people at Psychic Light for teaching me more about doing readings and to Alan Cox for the chance to do radio work. I also want to say a big thank you to Liz for my experience with PartyLite. You helped me get over my fear of working in public.

In the past few years I've also been involved with a group of ArchAngels. They connected me with Jan, who has encouraged, dragged and persuaded me to give these beings a voice in the world. Thank you Jan. That journey has only just begun. I'm sure we will have more to do when the time is right.

Finally, I have Helen and Jan to thank for my blogs. Without your support these words would still be stuck in my head. Thank you also to Fiona, my editor, who has waited patiently for this birth. I would also like to mention Fiona, Natalie, Linda, Kathleen and my daughter for keeping faith with me every time I struggled with doubt. Your tough love and inspiration has carried me many times. Your generosity is endless.

As I have already said this list is not exhaustive. To each and every person who has shared my journey I am grateful for you company every step of the way.

WHY WRITE AT ALL?

"Inside each of us is a voice waiting and wanting to be heard. That part that has been hidden, repressed, held back. It is where the truth lies. Somewhere between the Light and Dark."

What other people say

A Definition: Intuitive Senses

Why Write at All?

Much as I love all the stuff about the 'woo woo' side of being a psychic, it really isn't the way I live. Having reached a stage in my life where things have to be simple - senior moments are lurking around the corner - and preferring to be down to earth about what I do, I've taken on a challenge to write a blog a day.

Immediately there is a problem. I have a book full of the first two paragraphs of blog posts. They never seem to get finished. There is always something else I find I need to give my attention to. Even my first go this evening had to stop so I could make my daughter a meal, then run off to my Centre to open for someone using a room and finally off to my local Spiritualist church to chair for the medium doing the service. Now, I'm feeling the pressure! I promised myself and I want to do this yet getting the focus is hard.

What to write about? The question I've just answered, very briefly, about synchronicity? The chat I had with someone this evening about why their particular loved one didn't come through in a reading? The social media posting I do to encourage people to find the positive in every situation - no matter how difficult that might seem? The Reiki meditation I did to send out healing? There are many things that fall under the general titles of medium or psychic. So the easiest thing is to write about my day, every day for the next month. Sorry in advance if it gets boring but hopefully at the end you will see that my life is really no different than anyone else. Oh, OK then, perhaps the same with a few extraordinary bits added in, lol. - 17th November 2015.

That's how I set out late in 2015 to write. As a challenge to myself. Also, because I was rather fed up with people getting the wrong end of the stick about what a 'psychic' life is like. In actual fact, it's really a lot like any other life. With a few added bits, of course, that tend to make for an interesting time every now and again. They also mean that I'm an expert at changing my plans and going with the flow. When you step into the choices represented by your intuitive senses there are times when you just 'know' what to do, with whom and when. That's the bit that people often think of a 'woo woo'. And the bit I love!

I've always enjoyed books and writing. For a long time, I kept notes, poems, random inspirations on scraps of paper shoved into the books I was reading. I treated myself to fancy notebooks and jotted away whenever an idea grabbed me. I was, and always will be, a big fan of David Bowie. I remember watching a documentary in the seventies by the BBC where he explained how he wrote his songs. He appeared to be a bit tongue in cheek about writing a verse, cutting it up and rearranging the word or lines around. Yet whatever he was doing worked. His music matched my teenage angst - mixed up, muddled up and confused. I was fascinated to try this way of writing after spending many happy but frustrating hours trying to capture my thoughts and feelings in poems that didn't scan. Writing was an exploration. A way of saying complicated sounding simple things so others might understand. It was an adventure.

Entering adult life I ended up doing a lot of writing for my corporate job - plans, project briefs, press releases, letters, case notes. Over time these sucked all the fun out of writing. Writing became hard work, a bit of a bind. My love for words stopped. Sentences, paragraphs and pages ground to a halt as inspiration ceased to flow. Then writing became a chore, slowly but surely, as I drafted and redrafted. The meaning of what was being written was made to fit with conventions, structure and form once more. Eventually I stopped completely. I only wrote when studying or working. My voice was being lost. That became a real issue. All the joy in writing was kept from me for such a long time that I missed one of the ways I could express myself.

Through my blogging I've realised that people still have lots of questions about what being psychic means. There is a lot of misunderstanding about what it's like to work with Spirit people and Guides. Even some doubt about who can make these connections and how to do it. From the idea that it's a gift from a Divine Being given only to a few to the idea that I must be very brave because ghosts are scary. All sorts of perceptions about me and my work get thrown into the mix. The most interesting reactions followed my regular posting of a daily blog. Thankfully most people seemed to be slightly relieved that I appeared to be just like them. A fairly normal, busy, working woman doing her thing. Then the questions started to come in. Along with the feedback that what I was writing about was helpful to the people who were reading it. That's when I recognised that inside my blogs was a book waiting to get out. Something to explain; to be helpful; to be thought-provoking; and, to speak for the Spirit people in a down to earth way.

It was at this point that I started a debate with myself. Words like medium, clairvoyant and psychic are understood in a stereotypical way. They are a short cut description of something. But the associated ideas they are connected with don't necessarily fit with my experiences of working with Spirit people. They are also words that produce strong reactions from people. And open the door for lots of misunderstanding. My blogs have shown me the importance of using clear, straightforward language to describe what I do. If we all spoke with the same meaning it would be much simpler. So I started to talk about my intuitive senses. My life runs on intuition – what I feel – rather than logic – what I think. My feelings are the reflection of the energy I sense around me. That's what my psychic senses do. We all have intuition – that gut feeling – so I pay more attention to it than perhaps most people. It's what led me into the world and life I'm leading now. And I realised I had the title for my book with a way I could write it.

In deciding to step up to the challenge to myself by turning my blog into a book I've also found the joy of writing again. Ideas bounce in and out of my mind all day. It's fun to sit down in my quiet time and find out which ones are going to emerge as I flow s piece of writing. I'm back to scraps of paper, random notes and jottings stuffed into my diary. I want to share what an intuitive psychic world is really like so that more people will be encouraged to explore their natural intuitive abilities too. I'm also back to trying the David Bowie way of assembling things. My writing is exciting again.

Talking involves both speaking and listening. Writing is the same. I'm speaking by sharing my words. You are listening by reading them. If you understand what I'm saying then let's have a conversation. You don't have to agree with me and I don't have to agree with you. What matters is that we are thinking about, talking about and discussing how we understand the meaning of our lives. Who knows, we might even find we agree more than we expect to.

I hope you enjoy our conversation!

Annie Conboy

What other people say

"There are times in your life when you need a certain kind of help, support and guidance that isn't the tried and tested. Yet you can't put your finger on what that is at the time, but when it comes along you just know it's exactly right. Meeting Annie Conboy was exactly right for me. I was stuck, feeling lost and had to make some decisions about my future. Annie has this incredible ability to bring all that is stuck to the surface and allow it out into the open with great warmth and humour. It is no exaggeration when I say that with Annie I am transforming my life in so my ways. I can feel my confidence growing and am beginning to stand in my own light and that's all down to the work I've been doing with Annie." *Paula*

"Annie has an amazing gift! Apart from always being kind and having a nice word of support, she's such an inspiration, so knowledgeable, and she always gave me so much insight, reassurance, direction and encouragement through all the years I've known her. I always come away feeling empowered and lifted. She works with compassion and integrity, and is extremely honest. Thank you Annie, for everything, today & always! *Silvia*

"You are the reason I live in beautiful Wales with your wise words of advice you changed my life I will be eternally grateful xxxx" *Linda*

I was troubled a few days ago and went down to meet this beautiful lady! We had a heart to heart discussion. I had to make an important decision that night and was struggling to fight head -heart…The woman strengthened me and I felt calm and confident again. I made the decision and once change happened that thick cloud of negativity uneasiness left my abode! Moreover, she was so kind… she didn't charge me for the consultation, instead gave me a warm hug. What a beautiful soul." *Sylvia*

"I would like to say: The best kind of people are the ones that come into your life and make you see the sun where once you saw clouds. The people that believe in you so much you start to believe that too. The people that love you simply for being you. The once in a lifetime kind of people." *Silvia*

"I've known Annie Conboy for a while now, lovely woman. She saw a light in me and I felt as though she took me under her wing, guided and protected me. I attended many of her groups and courses of which I learnt each time, not only of everything metaphysical but life's challenges too. I have since moved away from the UK to Australia but keep in close contact. Whenever I need help even now she'll help me nut through a problem. I call her one of my spiritual teachers." *Andreas*

A Definition: Intuitive Senses

Claresentience: the ability to feel or sense energy vibrations relating to another's feelings or physical conditions. Experienced by sensations in the intuitive person's own body. Sometimes as if they had that feeling or physical sensation themselves.

Clarevoyance: the ability to see people, places and objects not physically present, in the mind's eye or as if present. The images can be from the past, present or future.

Clareaudiance: the ability to hear the voices of people not physically present, or sounds that have no physical cause as if in the mind or externally. The voices and sounds can be from the past, present or future.

Clarecognisense: the ability to have a clear thought or knowing about a piece of information that has entered your head. It is not connected to anything you may have been thinking and can appear as a random, possibly intrusive, thought.

Clarealliance: the ability to sense a non-physical smell as if it was bring picked up by the nose.

Claregustance: the ability to taste a non-physical substance as if it was in the mouth being sensed by tastebuds.

A PLACE TO START

"Start from where you are. There is no other point that will make sense." Captain Jack

My brief history of Spirit, Spirituality and Spiritualism …

And finally, before I begin, there is one more explanation

Becoming psychic

My brief history of Spirit, Spirituality and Spiritualism ...

I realise that some of the things I'm going to be writing about might not make sense unless I give a little bit more background information about what I understand of my Spirit, our spirituality and Spiritualism. I suppose I'm condensing about thirty or forty years of reading down into one quick chapter. Not much of a challenge! Of course, the best way to understand is to go and do the reading for yourself. But you might not have time or energy to plough through all the different points of view that have been expressed on these subjects. I am more than happy if you want to challenge what I say in this explanation. I hope you come to know that I love questions and debate. (You can email me at admin@annieconboy.net) The rebel in me often wants to fire up the rebel in other people. But please remember, this is my view, my choice of what I've picked out and my way of making sense of humanity's search for the meaning of existence. Everyone needs to find their own way.

Where do I start? Do I pick the Big Bang theory. Or the Bible. Actually, I want to start somewhere else. I need to present the information I am certain of because of my intuitive connections. So I'm starting with Spirit. To the best of my understanding I am a human being with a physical body, energy aura and a Spirit that makes the other two parts conscious and breathing. If the Spirit is not connected to the body and aura I'm dead. Even if the body can be kept alive by technology. My Guides have been very clear that my Spirit, my consciousness, is the eternal part of me. I will live for ever but not in any solid, stuck energy form. It is the Spirit part of me that travels between this Earth experience and the Afterlife. In the Afterlife I return to my Soul Group.

A Soul Group is made up of the energy consciousness of hundreds of spirits. Perhaps thousands. The group is together because each consciousness is vibrating at the same level of energy. Or in other words, each spirit in the Soul group is sharing the same sort of experiences. When my Guides started answering my questions about Spirit and Soul and what was the difference they showed me an image of the human brain. They smiled as they asked me to imagine I was a single cell in the mind of the Divine. One cell on its own has limitations; if I am connected to other cells we form a purpose. Perhaps we are the cells that process what the eyes are seeing... Or we could be the group of cells decoding the sounds we hear. Perhaps we are the cells who get all excited at the taste of chocolate. I like the idea of being the cell who gets to decode the taste of chocolate! Each area of the brain has a different function but all work together to process and store knowledge.

I love the idea that being human might be about taking part in the Divine thought experiment. I can get that idea. Many scientists use thought experiments to test their theories before they try them in the material world. I also love the idea that I am part of a bigger group. The Spirit that is in my human body has a purpose. I am making a contribution to shared knowledge or experiences.

However, I feel that in trying to make sense of our reason for being here, we have gone a bit off track. Back in the mists of time the idea of the Divine emerged. I am not asking you to believe that a Divine Being, or more than one, exists but some of us are more comfortable with that idea.

That is where the idea of spirituality starts to have an impact. I believe we all share a yearning for a deeper connection to something. To each other. Even to something greater than our individual selves. This idea that the sum is greater than all the parts leads us back to the model of the brain. It functions within the body as the overall co-ordinator, yet it's made up of many billions of little, individual bits. All those little bits must work together as much as possible to enable things to get done. In this search for connection we have to overcome, appease or get around the natural force that pushes us to ensure our own survival first. So we move towards altruistic acts. To being selfless. Wanting to help or make things better. In this we are guided by those around us, supported by the emotions of love and kindness, and encouraged by the way it feels good to act in collaboration with other people. Team efforts show us the rewards of working as one.

With the emergence of a Divine Being it becomes easier to ask everyone to put in the effort of cooperating. There is a sense of purpose that arises from the idea of getting some sort of Divine reward. Unfortunately, it is also easy to bend the efforts of a large group people into less caring and sharing paths. Especially if the energy of the Divine becomes concentrated in only a small bunch of special people. The interpreters of the common good remove the need for people to tune in for themselves. It becomes easier to step out of being responsible for the actions taken. The Divine can be the one to blame. The Divine is the one at fault. And the Divine is the one causing all of the woes of the world. I feel that by the start of the Industrial Revolution (early in the nineteenth century) spirituality had become something that was said rather than done.

It was at this point that a new phenomenon appeared. Spiritualism. Only it wasn't called that at first. In 1848 the Fox sisters began communicating with an apparently non-physical being (See 'The Unwilling Martyrs' by Mariam Buckner Pond for example). A ghost. A Spirit presence that kept the whole family awake at night, night after night unless they communicated with it. As the news of the nightly visitations spread, many religious people visited the property and came away convinced that the ghost was communicating with the family. It began a wave of interest in all things psychic. Finally it developed into what we now call Spiritualism. The belief that it is possible to contact the Spirits of the dead. Of course, this was a rather destabilising idea for established western religions.

Over the last 100 years a fierce debate has raged between those who believe you can contact the dead and those who think you can't. It's the debate I stepped into as a sceptic when I first began to realise I might be receiving contact from non-physical beings. What I do know from my personal experiences is that I can have conversations with beings who have no physical body. They have personalities, habits and memories that are completely separate from mine, and ideas and beliefs that certainly don't match mine. And they can tell me things about the person sitting in front of me that I have no way of knowing. I have considered telepathy, lucky guessing, cold reading and all sorts of techniques by which I'm supposed to have got the the information. What persuaded me was the consistency. Time and again I have said something in all innocence only to find that it is a defining piece of evidence for the person I'm passing it on to!

So why are the Spirit people making all of this effort? Aren't we getting on okay with living without them? Even if our faith in a Divine Being is fading away, there are still people trying to do things for the greater good. I guess our record stands for itself. War, more war and even more war. It's become possible to wipe out vast numbers of human beings without pausing to consider if this is what a Divine Being really wants from us. Co-operation to solve things has become a background option. In the foreground is aggression, possession and greed. It is as if this wonderful brain that can achieve so much has pressed the self-destruct button. Or at least got very sick. So the Spirit people come back to remind us about love. To reconnect us to each other. And to encourage us to find better ways for our children's children's children. Somehow they also picked me. A sceptic full of world weary cynicism. They contacted me, shook me up and reminded me about all the good things that happen when we work for each other. It's for them that I finally decided to write about my life. Because I'm no different from anyone else. Yet I'm trying to be better than I was.

And finally, before I begin, there is one more explanation …

Over a long period of time I've had a chance to think about what counts as real. Is it what I can touch, taste, smell and see? Or is it what I can feel, think and sense? Because I can sense far more than my physical senses tell me is there. I've looked at all sorts of theories about reality. Some of them quite tough for me to grasp because anything with maths in it sends me into a panic. I've done my research because I've come across a lot of people who tell me that the world I experience isn't real. The heart attack pain I experienced from one of the Spirit people was impossible. The memories of deceased loved ones who share them with me are good guesses. The detailed information I provide is due to searching on the internet.

 At first I was frustrated, because to me these experiences were no different than the things that happen in my everyday life. They were also accurate. So, what was going on? Going back to science was my first impulse because I have always tended to trust science to explain things. Yet there is disagreement even within science about the nature of reality. That's when I started to ask my Guides for more understanding. I wanted to know how the intuitive world works. Especially as I was planning to live in it full time. I suppose I wanted to be able to believe that what I was experiencing had some validity. Then I would trust it.

Over a period of months my Guides presented me with step by step lessons about the energy world. A different way of understanding the nature of reality that was helpful to me. Sometimes in this book I will be talking about connections and intuition in terms of energy, so, I would like you to see the world as I see it by explaining the nature of energy.

It's my belief that human beings are a duality. Two parts made up of two energies. I also believe that over time we shift from one part to another and from one energy to another. That's because being an energy being is all about movement and flow. Energy is not static. There is always some movement although it might be so slow as to seem like it is solid. The parts we have are Spirit and Physical.

The Physical lives when the spirit meshes with it and dies when the spirit departs. Another possible way to think of this is that there is a feminine energy and a masculine energy. The feminine energy is a creative force. The masculine energy is a 'make it so' force. We need both so that ideas are translated into action. That is how human beings live – by taking action.

As energy we can connect with each other. That is what intuitive psychic senses are based on. Translating the interactions of energies shared between us. However the focus is often on the Physical part of ourselves. It has the slowest energy so appears mostly as a solid form. The more fluid, faster moving energy of the aura is often unnoticed. Most of us lose the connection, so to speak, between Spirit and Physical because the Spirit information flows through the aura and we no longer process it. Our heads are too full of our day to day lives. Yet enough breaks through from time to time to puzzle us. That gut instinct about something. The thought that I haven't seen someone for a while and then I bump into them. Knowing that the phone is going to ring and who will be on the other end of the line. That random déjà vu moment of feeling like I've experienced this before. Feeling that someone is ill, hurt or in distress and finding out it's true. Lots of little connections that make us wonder. It's the subtle exchange of energy going on between all of us.

Opening up to my intuitive senses allows me to process all of that energy flow. I can know things without being told. Also knowing without using telepathy. I am aware of what is most likely to happen to me. There is a leading edge to the energy flow that is just ahead of me in this moment of experiencing time. If I pay attention to the information that is there, I am looking into my own future. Or the future of other people. I don't need anything to translate the energy. It happens automatically now that I have instructed my brain to pay attention to the signals.

Human beings are not the only energy around. There are plenty of non-physical beings who can contact us by exchanging energy with us. That is how I discovered Spirits, Angels and Elementals. They are alongside us in the energy. Sharing our energy in an effort to communicate with us. As they did with me once I started to pay attention to what my intuitive mind was saying.

Becoming psychic

I guess you could call me a late developer. Although I experienced the New Age movement of the 1960s and '70s, as a teenager I was much more interested in boyfriends, boy bands and fashion. I did have a passion for wanting to understand what made people tick. I was also fascinated by science and scientific enquiry. I was sure that I could discover all I needed to know about people and life if I studied psychology. The occult, seances, table tipping and ghosts seemed irrational. As did auras, energy waves and UFOs. Oh, such youthful contempt! I've been blessed with a journey over the last twenty-five years that turned all of that teenage certainty upside down. Yet I stayed a sceptic until the last possible moment. The moment when I recognised my fall to Earth, my reasons for being here and the new direction my life was taking. The day I understood that the Spirit World was actually picking me to be on the team.

So, what was happening to me? Had I finally gone off on a ramble into a world of fantasy? My first recognisable contact came from feeling their energy. I felt like I was tingling all over or had suddenly developed goosebumps. At the time, I wasn't sure what this feeling was but it seemed to keep happening. I had read about psychic senses - most people seemed to talk about seeing and hearing Spirit - so I was left wondering what was really going on. Was this what 'they' called claresentience? I have to say 'they' still included my very judgemental stereotypes of the stranger portrayals of mediums. My sceptical mind wanted more proof that these feelings weren't random, that there was some intelligence behind them and that it really was caused by something other than myself. I began saying thank you in my mind whenever I felt the tingles. I admit I felt strange doing so. Some of the books I had read suggested that if you acknowledged what was happening it would make it happen more often. Strangely enough (or not!) I found that the more I said thank you the more the tingles happened.

Then I started looking for a way I could remove my own disbelief about mediumship. Only in acknowledging what I was experiencing would I be able to step into a world that was radically different from the world I was brought up in. I remember reading as many books as I could, going to see mediums in churches week in and week out, watching everything I could find on TV. There was a lot of conflicting information. It seemed as if there was no clear, simple way to understand how spirit communication worked. No matter how many questions I asked of people I found their explanations contradictory. I felt like I kept hitting a brick wall with my head. What were the straightforward explanations of my experiences? What did it all mean? And, more importantly, would I have to stop being sceptical if someone could explain it all logically to me?

Of course, by this time I was hooked. I suspect that was the plan all along. As I really wanted to work out what I was experiencing one night I sat down determined to get more than tingles. Sitting in my comfy chair, gathering all my courage, I asked if there was anyone there. I have to say that if anyone had answered 'yes...' I would have run a mile. The old, old social conditioning of a religious background still existed somewhere deep inside of me so I was scared. Really scared. But curious too. And stubborn. I wanted answers even if it turned out I had gone mad. What I felt was a warm tingle on the back of my right hand. The tingle became a feeling of pressure as if someone had gently touched the back of my hand. The pressure got stronger. It was unmistakable. Something or someone was touching my hand. Somehow I had the presence of mind to ask 'if that's you, please touch the back of my other hand'. The pressure on my right hand stopped. My left hand began to tingle on the back. The same gentle pressure of a touch was there, exactly where I had asked it to be. I was holding my breath by now. Saying thank you again I asked if whoever was there could touch my right shoulder. So they did. Then my face. And they did. By this time I was shaking with excited amazement. I sat for a long time alternating between belief and disbelief at the feel of that touch.

Once I got used to the touch on my hand, which seemed to come in rather randomly at times, I wanted to find out who was doing it. This is where claresentience gets challenging, frustrating and annoying. We are so used to seeing and hearing the world, rather than feeling, that we haven't got a language for feelings as detailed as the words we can use to describe the sights and sounds we experience. I could tell it was a touch but what was that touch meant to convey to me? It became a guessing game. Did a touch on the shoulder mean well done? Or don't worry? Or steady on? What about the feeling of sadness that came across me? Or of anger? Or of love? I was still no nearer to knowing who was communicating and what they were trying to tell me.

Fortunately my Guides are a tough lot. They had finally got me paying attention and weren't prepared to let me slip away again. They sent me a light bulb moment. Sitting feeling frustrated with the touch on the back of my hand - something so amazing only a short while ago - I said 'if it's you help me find a yes or no response'. Instantly the touch changed to what felt like two taps on the back of my hand. Remembering all of the stuff I'd read about seances I asked 'if that is yes do two taps again'. Of course, there were two taps again. I had found a way to get information from the communicator. I was delighted. No more misunderstanding for me then. Then I realised that it would only work on questions that could be answered with yes or no. Multiple choice or either/or questions had no chance of being answered. Perhaps a hollow victory then? I realised I needed more help.

The next sessions of contact were hard going. I didn't know what to ask, there were lots of questions with too many answers and I was uncertain that I was picking up the right number of taps. After a particularly frustrating evening I wrote in my notes GIVE UP! Fortunately, the next day there I was again sitting ready to communicate. I had decided to ask for a different way to get yes and no. I also had a long list of questions I'd drawn up to keep me going and speed up the process. When I felt the pressure on the back of my hand I asked that the yes signal be changed to a touch on my right hand and the no signal be a touch on my left hand. Then I started with my list: Are you male; are you female; are you family to me; are you friend to me; are you a Guide? The game of 20 questions went on for some time. At the end of it I had worked out that the male energy who was with me was my Guide and that we knew each other in some way. It was exciting. At last I was getting somewhere.

Encouraged by this clear message I continued to work through sessions of asking questions. I found that as I worked I understood the meaning of what I felt more. There came a point, when I was getting a touch on my hand, that I suddenly seemed to know the answer in my head too. It was as if I had an answer slightly before I asked the question in my mind. What had happened was that by developing my claresentience I had also started to improve my clarecognisence (direct knowing). This breakthrough really energised me. I put more effort into my development than ever before. However, I often felt like there was still something missing. It was clear that I could get information but what was the point? I had no idea how it worked, why and what I was supposed to do with what I was being told. It was time to take my search outside what I could achieve sitting on my own.

As ever, my Guides had a plan. At that time I was doing market research for a job. One day I was out and about knocking on doors as usual. At one house, a lovely couple offered me a cup of tea. We fell into a discussion about gardening. They asked me if I wanted to take away a plant in a pot – they were downsizing. I have brown thumbs but will willing take any plant in need of rescue. They just have to be tough to survive my care. At that point the couple apologised that the pot contained a stone with some painting on it. It had been donated by their friend who decorated stones. Wondering exactly what could be on the stone for them to feel a bit anxious I said that was no problem. I left after a pleasant chat with my completed form and new plant. Once I got home I had a closer look at the stone. On it was painted "Colne Spiritualist Church". Laughing I realised my Guides were determined to lead me onwards.

When I called the Spiritualist church I spoke to a wonderful gentleman called Colin. He told me about the church and what times the services were. He also invited me to go along to a service and speak to him if I wanted to learn more. My Guides had found me exactly the best Earth Guide to talk to on my first contact with a Spiritualist church. I went along to the next service and eventually joined a development group there. Though I wasn't sure it got any clearer in the early days of the group. Everyone seemed to 'see' things, one or two were able to 'hear' words but no one else seemed to 'feel' connections. I persevered. In every exercise I felt more and more. Then, as I began to trust what I was experiencing, I grew more confident at passing on the information to my classmates. Listening to them confirming the accuracy of what I was saying I felt encouraged. Then, finally, my connections improved enough for my Guides to step forward more strongly as well.

My Guides explained why, what and how the connection to the Spirit World works. They also arranged to bounce me into demonstrating my mediumship publicly. Then they really piled it on by asking me to start teaching about intuition, psychic senses and mediumship. 'Who me?' I squeaked. 'I'm not sure…' I squeaked again. Not me. No way. No chance. Of course, I should have known that the Guide team would find a way to hook me in. They always do.

Today I have all the 'clares' to a stronger or lesser degree and teach many people who start with only one sense up and running. I guess that's the point of this book. I would like to share some of my everyday experiences so that you can also find a way to explore your intuition. My reason for wanting this is that I'm sure once you understand what skills you have you will want to apply them. You might even find that when you use your intuitive ability you help other people as a result. I want you to know that what we can do is as far away from 'woo woo' as it possibly could be. Using these senses can change your life dramatically and for the better. I know that in the last 11 years, since I really embraced what I was able to do, I have been happier than I ever thought possible. This is a gift everyone can have. I love my intuitive life.

In the following chapters I want to explain to you why my world has changed by being an intuitive medium. That first set of tingles from the Spirit World has brought me a long, long way!

ALL ABOUT ME

"Life shapes you. Life almost breaks you.
Then Life remakes you anew. In between the gaps you lose the old
and gain the true you."

All about me

Mid Life Crisis

Life picks up pace

Spirit moves in

About me

I was born into a real 'Coronation Street'. A row of back to back
terraced houses on the fringes of Oldham Edge. A small but
independent community of people trying to make their way in
life. My Nanna and Granddad lived around the corner. My aunty
and uncle still lived at home with them. Everyone knew everyone
else. They mostly worked in the local mills together. There wasn't
much privacy and there was a strong religious belief that ensured
everyone was willing to help everyone else out.

I remember the ice on the inside of the windows on a winter's
morning, how cold the lino felt getting out of bed. And yes, we
did have our parent's coats over us on the bed to keep us warm.
Running downstairs to the warmth of the fire that Mum had lit, we
had slices of bread for breakfast. I guess you might have thought
of us as poor. But I didn't feel deprived of anything. I had a loving
mother and father and two brothers. We went to Ireland in the
summer and I got to play on a farm. My other grandfather and
grandmother were older. There were more uncles and an aunt. It
was a different world compared to my home town.

In fact, I had lots of aunties. The whole street knew who I was and
looked out for me and my brothers. As a tomboy it meant that I
was often told that girls didn't do things like climb eight foot high
walls, or trees, or swing on rope. They don't roam around the Edge,
our tiny little bit of moor in the centre of town, jumping in puddles.
Or watch motorbikes doing rally cross. Girls in dresses don't get
to drive wagons or diggers. They don't have swords and defeat
armies. And they certainly don't lead their little brothers on all sorts
of escapades either. My Mum must have despaired of me. She kept
making dresses for me and I kept destroying them. I often think she
should have put me in trousers. However, in my childhood that was
something girls couldn't do either.

I'm sure the neighbours looked on in sympathy. Whatever I was told
I couldn't or shouldn't do, I did. My rebel head clicked in and I was
off. I was the leader of all sorts of mischief. The only time I would

behave somewhat more like a girl was on a Sunday. Then I got to wear a pretty dress and go to church. My wise parents always took us into a side chapel where there was a door for a quick escape with a noisy child. We also got to take toys to play with, as long as we were quiet. Most of this went over my head. Church was a place I put up with because I could wear a party dress. My favourite was a black velvet one with white lace on the collar and sleeves. Also, it was a place where everyone told me how lovely I was. I bet my mother raised her eyebrows at this all the time.

In Ireland, my grandfather's farm was at the end of the road. I used to roam around with the sheepdogs or pick berries for jam. I was fascinated with watching my Dad skin a rabbit or milk a cow. We had fresh soda bread every day with home-made butter and jam. In the evening we played cards or my Dad played songs on his accordion. My uncle joined him and played clarinet or saxophone. We sang along, danced and clapped. My little gang got bigger as my cousins joined in all of the adventures. I loved the freedom from school, from supervision, from having to behave.

Back in England we moved to live in the shop across the road when I was about five. Our old house was rented out. Then the house next door changed hands too. We had a group of Pakistani men in our street. They shared the house next door to my old one and went to work in the mills. They slept in shifts so there was a lot of coming and going. The smell of curry wafted around the street. Our little street suddenly seemed very exotic. I was fascinated. Especially as they didn't go to either of our churches. Not to the one right beside us where I regularly climbed the vicarage walls to get the apples from the tree. Or to the one I went to every Sunday. Going to church was a must. How interesting for me that there were people who didn't. I suspect this might have been my first discovery that people could believe different things. That there were different Gods.

When I was seven my Mum had a baby. Another boy. I had so wanted a sister to play with. Dolls had got to me by then. I had so many given as Christmas and birthday presents that I started to play with them more than footballs. My Mum liked me playing with dolls. For a start, I wasn't ruining my clothes quite as much. I was also starting to be interested in babies, getting married and cooking. She was torn between recognising my curiosity and intelligence and the traditional expectations of a safe life as an adult woman. She had felt the restrictions of being intelligent but with very little on offer for career choices. She had worked in the mill office before having me but unless you were a widow and had to work, or single and childless, you stayed at home to look after your children. My Mum taught me to read before I went to school. She loved books and that's where she lost herself when real life became just too much. I'm sure she hoped for so much more for me as an adult even if she couldn't see how it might come about.

By the time I was nine I was working hard to pass my Eleven Plus so I could go to grammar school. Mum put in extra hours with me to help. At the same time, she had another baby, my sister at last, and she and my Dad were busy every spare hour building a new house. His business as a demolition contractor was doing well and building us a home was his dream. We moved away from our Coronation Street to the more middleclass area of Thornham. It was a completely different world. A detached house surrounded by gardens and fields. To me it was much more like being in Ireland. The tomboy came back with a vengeance as I explored all over the place. There was one drawback though. I was old enough to help with my baby sister but selfish enough to want to roam free. It was a challenge. Boarding school became an active consideration for me if I passed my exams.

Around this time, I also began to wonder about my religious beliefs. I had been through all of the processes – Baptism, Holy Communion, Confirmation. Did I really believe in one God, one male who seemed to be either angry or peaceful depending on which bit of the Bible I read? What about the people I knew who didn't have a God like that? As with a lot of my changes of direction I thought about it for a long time. In our house there was no way I could opt out of our religion, and then, when I passed my exam,

I went to a Catholic school. Boarding school turned out not to be an option because of cost. So I followed in my Mum's footsteps and went to a girls' only school. I loved Notre Dame but I felt more restrictions piling on. Mostly good ones I suspect and with the best of intentions. The Sisters wanted to educate the daughters of the poor so that we could go on to have better life choices. A large proportion of my classmates went on to university or careers. In one way my mother's plan worked. I got a good education. Life was all laid out in front of me to pick what I wanted to do. I had options.

What I did was fell in love. I was Juliet and he was Romeo. My Dad said we couldn't be engaged if I was still at school, even if it was the sixth form. So, of course, I left school as soon as I had a job. Being an office clerk by day and doing part time study at night I still hoped to achieve my dream of some sort of university place. I did practical courses for the first couple of years. Then my interest in what makes people tick kicked in and I started to read more about psychology. That turned out to be another challenge to my ideas about religion or, as it now seemed to have become, spirituality. Perhaps the influences of the 1960s and 70s New Age movements were a part of this too. For someone from a family committed, at least outwardly, to a set of rather rigid beliefs, meeting people who lived by a very different set of rules was mind expanding. I wondered why people needed religion in the first place. The rebel was still alive in me.

For a long time, though, the rebel took a back seat. I married my first love. We settled into a pattern followed by our parents and their parents before them. I went to work, we went on holidays, we had a mortgage and responsibilities. My father-in-law died a year after we married. My religious beliefs didn't seem to help deal with our grief. There were a stormy few years to ride out. All the time I was searching to understand the human mind. There were no answers in the outer world that made any sense to me. It all seemed to be book theories. Real people didn't act the way the books implied. So, my search continued through a challenging break up and into a new relationship. I still hadn't found what I was looking for. The girl from the terraced streets still wanted an explanation. Why was life like this? Why were people like this? What was the point?

Mid Life Crisis

As I stepped into my thirties I finally began to follow the road inward. It was a journey to a fairly new place. I know I went inward in my teenage years. Friendships were hard to find. Romantic love coloured all of my dreams. Becoming an adult took me a long time even though I married, worked and got on with the day to day of life. The urge to go back inside myself became very strong, especially when I started to feel the ticking of my biological clock. Although I was, as I thought, pursuing a career, something shifted as I got to 35. I started to want or even need to have a baby. However, I wasn't in any kind of situation where that could happen. Or not unless I made some big changes. It was my first full on encounter with my creative force. My work was all about masculine energy. To feel so driven by feminine urges was a bit of a shock. It probably scrambled my brain for quite a while. I know it seemed to scramble my body. And it certainly didn't seem to be something I could turn off.

That inner wandering pushed me through a couple of unsuccessful relationships. I was also getting more and more work dropped on me. Driving up and down the country, going from here to there, I thought I was building a career. I was actually on a hamster wheel going around and round but couldn't get off. In truth, I don't feel I wanted to get off. The rebel in my head was rushing in where angels would certainly have feared to tread. That old drive – girls can't do that – had me hitting my head against a toughened glass ceiling. Having to outperform my male colleagues and still being thought not quite good enough became a huge frustration. I was operating firmly from the extreme of my masculine energy. That's ok for a tomboy but even tomboys get tired and bored. I wanted to be soft and fluffy for a bit. My inner journey needed to hurry up and get me to a point of balance but I was definitely dragging my feet.

More and more my life became hard work. I'm sure my Guides were wishing I could stop putting myself into a toxic work environment. I hated having to flatter people to get things done. I hated having to put on a set of balls wrapped in pink velvet just to get taken seriously. It was horrid to feel the uncertainty of what to be. I couldn't ever really be one of the boys but I also rejected being the nurturing tea maker for all and sundry. Like my challenges with religion, my work seemed to offer no real place for my creative skills to be recognised appropriately. It was a black period in my life. Now I feel the only light bits were the chances I got to tinker with my spirituality, though I know I was only playing around the edges. The sceptic in me kept pulling me back from diving in deeper.

I moved from job to job within my organisation. I was chasing a dream but it seemed far out of reach. One of my moves involved working away in London during the week while spending weekends at the other end of the country in Newcastle. It was exhausting so often I stayed in my lodgings instead. My landlady, Margaret, was on her own with three children and we got on well. We had a few nights out together and there was a lot of chat and laughter. Margaret introduced me to reading cards. She had found a book at the library so showed me with a pack of ordinary playing cards. Her life had been very interesting as far as I was concerned. She had explored more of the spiritual side of life, had lived abroad and taken the big decision to raise her children by herself. The way the cards seemed to be able to predict was tested again and again. I got my own book and cards. I did a card spread most days. Most days the cards turned out to have been spot on.

I was really testing myself. I was sure the results had more to do with random chance and vague meanings than any actual ability to tell the future but I was hooked. Like a scientist I was trying the experiment again and again to see how often the results confirmed my scepticism. That was my reductionist brain busy denying that there might be anything in the turn of a card that could actually be correct. If it was possible for the cards to predict what was coming up I would have to shift my world view. And I would also have to find out why and how it happened. Of course, I'm no different than most people. We are introduced to the 'scientific' method very early in life. It's a useful technique for solving problems, thinking we are controlling outcomes and finding facts to help us feel we understand the world. We do need to understand our world. Unfortunately, more often than not the scientific view has become locked down into a sense that if it can't be proved by repetition then it can't be true. The cards were very often right. Yet sometimes they were definitely wrong. The book was rather unclear about how the cards managed to be predictive. There was no real explanation of what might be happening to influence the cards. Was it me? If so, how? As usual, I stuck to my experiments and resisted taking any significant steps to find out about my intuition.

When I got bored with my playing cards I invested in a Tarot pack. It was much harder to understand than I expected and I bought a few books to see if I could work it out. I couldn't! The result of that was I spent quite a lot of time rushing around to workshops, events and Mind, Body and Spirit Fairs wondering why I was there. I had a good friend who kept telling me I had a Native American Spirit Guide with me. Christine loved all the spiritual stuff. She talked to her Angels and Guides. She dragged a reluctant me all over the place. I am so grateful that she persevered. Attending these experiences, I was able to let myself get interested and more involved in several things that I had studied right through from my teenage years. So, past lives, astrology, paranormal experiences and auras came out from the closet. This period of finding out more seemed to hold my biological clock at bay too. I was fascinated. What was it about the vision quests, meditation and Tarot cards that responded to that flow of energy? Of course, I was a long way from understanding that we live an energy life wrapped inside a human life. Or that the secret was to turn that on its head. My inner path was still very new to me.

Then I had a moment of pure bliss. A perfect connection to something I felt was Divine. Encouraged by Christine I began to practice astral travel. Sometimes it happened when I was what I considered wide awake. To the amusement of both of us it even happened once whilst I was on the phone with her. I was still the doubting Thomas and she was in fits of laughter. So that I could get comfortable with these spontaneous experiences, I was practicing meditating. Not very successfully I have to say. My mind hated to step aside and shut up. I was far too nosy about what was happening around me. So I had to practice sitting quietly a lot.

One afternoon I got comfortable in an exasperated kind of way. I wasn't expecting to settle but was determined to stick to trying. I was in my lovely attic bedroom. It was warm. I put some quiet music on and sat down. Within a few seconds I had gone. Zooming up through the roof higher and higher into the sky. I looked down at my roof rather awed to be seeing it through a bird's eye view. I flew higher and higher out into the stars and vastness of space. Yet I knew my body was still sitting quietly on my attic floor. My journey sped up. I was moving towards a golden light that was growing bigger and bigger until it filled my vision. Then I felt a shift of direction. I was being pulled into the golden light on a slight downwards movement. Sinking into the light I realised I was a golden speck of light now. There was a wonderful sense of peace. I seemed to be part of an endless sea of specks of light. We were all drifting steadily in a current towards a very bright Light that seemed to be on a higher point above us.

As I focused on that point it was so bright I couldn't really see what was in the Light. It suddenly seemed that I yearned to be at one with whoever was inside it. That was where I was being carried. It's impossible to describe the flow of love I experienced. Every spark, including me, was radiating pure love towards each other and the Light. The Light was returning that love and adding to it. I knew I was in the presence of the Divine. I knew I never wanted to be anywhere else. I wanted to surge forward and join the Light. At that point I sensed a push backward. The 'No' came. I knew they wanted me to return to my Earth life. I resisted. I shouted that there was nothing left for me on Earth. I said I wouldn't go. The gentle, loving push continued. The feeling that I really had no choice and had to return to my attic. I was pleading not to be sent back. The warm, tough love surrounded me and I was pushed back out of that golden gateway. As if I had been catapulted I flew toward Earth and my body.

As I clicked back in I was crying. I knew that if they had let me stay I would have died here on Earth. An unexplained death. I was back to a life I didn't want. It took me a long time that evening to regain some balance. For me the experience was a powerful wake up call. My life felt empty. I had come to hate my work but believed that I had no other options because I had a mortgage to pay. I was single, not dating and still pestered by my biological clock. Yet I have never, before or since, felt such incredible bliss. It was like love magnified ten thousand times. Earthly love is only a pale shadow of what I felt. The closest I have ever come to that feeling is the love I feel for my daughter. Having glimpsed the Afterlife, I struggled with the disappointment of having to be human.

The second half of my thirties flew by as I searched for some kind of meaning in my life. I was suffering with burn out but not ready to admit it. I stuck stubbornly to my toxic habits. The bliss seemed so remote. For me it made being human harder. I guess I wanted to opt out of responsibility for making the life I had. I wouldn't change. My fear and resistance was too strong. Even after my vision I still clung to logic. There were no answers I wanted to acknowledge because that would mean starting a new life. In the end, I became depressed, in such deep despair that I tried to leave this life. But it seemed I was here for the duration. Waking up when I thought I wouldn't ever do so again was a big blast of cold water in my face. It seemed I was here whether I wanted to be or not. That morning changed my life as much as the vision did. Deep down I knew I would just have to get on with living. And whatever that might represent.

Still reluctant to walk away from my job I continued to be a part of the rat race, until I went on holiday with Christine. She insisted we get our cards read. I must have been one of the most challenging people the reader had that day. I was in my 'I'm not listening' mood. She told me quite distinctly that I needed to sit in a circle and develop my intuitive connections. She told me three times to check I understood. I did understand but I was still sulking from having to stay here so I ignored her. After the holidays, the Universe took a hand. I admit that I was being childish. I can see that now. Refusing to see how ill I was, preventing myself from getting spiritual help and running fast in the opposite direction I was self-destructing in another way. I know somewhere in my head there was an ego voice going 'Well I might have to be here but I don't have to enjoy it. So there!' But the only one suffering was me. So, the Universe turned my life upside down. I had a breakdown. That finally pushed me to get help. I had to leave my job.

Still unable to engage with my intuitive abilities at least I was free from working conditions that were harmful for me. Slowly I pulled my life into some sort of shape. I had been helped enormously by counselling so when I felt well enough I retrained as a counsellor myself. One really powerful aspect of the training was that I had to keep a journal. Writing things down got them out of my head. I saw the patterns of my life much more clearly. Using meditation and self-exploration I finally started to uncover the creative part of me. My imagination had room to breathe. Tumbling into my forties I was determined that life would begin again for me. I still had no idea where I was going but I was certainly much clearer who I was. Finding myself more open to consider what I believed about life, the Universe and everything but still stuck in the desire to be rational about it, a new chapter was definitely opening up.

Life Picks Up Pace

It seems that life was worth it after all. When I was 42 I gave birth to my daughter. All those years of searching for meaning were swept aside. I immersed myself in being with this new creation. She was perfect. My life took another direction as I grappled with the responsibility and joy of being a parent. I spent a lot of time with her because I didn't want to miss anything in her growing up. I felt that after such a long time of waiting, then getting to the point of believing I wouldn't have a child, her presence in my life was a blessing. So work went on the back burner to a greater extent and I spent my time being Mum.

As a mother it's normal to think your child is precious and special, to look for every single developmental stage as soon as possible. Or to worry if your child seems to be taking their time to learn a new skill. My world shrank quite a bit. I wanted the company of other mums. Baby talk. Planning about schools, activities and future talents. Was it normal that my child couldn't sleep more than three hours at a time? That she would fight off sleep like it was a life battle? That she stared at me with wise, old eyes as I tended to her? That she loved my crystals? But wouldn't talk? That she climbed everything she could? But wouldn't go near some people no matter how they encouraged her? And could do puzzles a much older child would find a challenge?

I relied on my own Mum to guide me too. She was amazing both as my Mum and a Granny. I learned to appreciate her in a very new and different way. Her advice was very simple. She encouraged me to listen to my own intuitions about my daughter. And to follow what I felt. She was confident that I could be a good mum even when I wasn't. Most of all she adored her newest grandchild. I can't explain how I felt when she died. My daughter was only two and a half but my Mum was struggling to stay here. Eventually her body gave up and Mum stepped across the rainbow bridge to the Afterlife. I know she would have stayed longer if she had been able to. But I felt orphaned. Abandoned even. I had a small child, a rocky relationship and the role of breadwinner. The light was my daughter.

My lovely baby and toddler was an amazing enigma. I'm sure I'm not the only mum to feel that about their child. After all, we are waiting for a new person to emerge and show themselves to the world. As I had a lot more knowledge about spiritual ideas I wondered at the regular, routine times she woke up every night. On one such occasion I saw two orbs dancing up and down the bed over her. And why she seemed able to tell who to smile at and who not to. My intuition was still rather slow at this time but I understood her choices. Some people had open hearts. Some didn't. Since she didn't talk I couldn't get an explanation. Though I knew she could talk. I'd heard the words over the baby monitor one day. Or so I thought. Until one day my friend gave me a funny look. What? I asked her. She asked if I was having a conversation with my daughter. Of course, I said, yes. But you are the only one speaking she replied. It made me think.

From that time I started to tell my toddler that down here we had to speak. Though she was stubborn. She only decided to talk after she turned three. And that was the point she started to sleep through the night too. Getting her to sleep was still an issue. Until I picked up on her Spirit Guides. They were all children. Her imaginary friends came every night to play with her at bedtime. I spent many nights in her room, tuning into their energies, hoping to find a way to keep them quiet. Finally I sensed an adult presence with them. They had a nursery maid who looked after them. Between her and me we eventually got all of the children, my daughter included, to understand about bed time. I finally started to sleep through the night again. Not bad after three years feeling like a zombie.

As my daughter launched into talking she shared details about her between-lives choices and why she came here. However, she also told me quite clearly that she would like to go back to where it was all pink and perfect. Those were her words. They stunned me because how could she know so much detail about heaven? Our little family group had no religion to speak of. It wasn't a topic we discussed. Yet her description of why it was pink and perfect fitted my definition of heaven. She wanted to go to the Pink Perfect as soon as possible. And she was serious about it too. Immediately was her preferred choice. It was so difficult for her to accept that she had to stay human until she had finished the jobs she came here to do. These conversations jumped me back to my spiritual search. It seemed my daughter's intuitive senses were very active. I wanted to understand more. After all, if she was going to have to navigate life that way I wanted to be able to help her.

Spirit moves in

One of the hardest cliffs I had to step off (aside from becoming a parent) was to trust the connection to Spirit Beings. Aside from my natural tendency to doubt until I have evidence (my logical, analytical mind) there was another point of resistance. My background and my social conditioning both say that hearing, seeing and sensing Spirit is frightening, wrong, and the way to end up mentally ill. So, a leap of faith was required!

The religion of my birth would certainly say my ability to connect with spirits is the imaginings of a tortured mind. Being a woman is also somewhat of a barrier. There were and still are so many conventions about how I have to be in the world, mostly based on keeping a low profile and knowing my place. To imagine that I might actually have a natural ability and could be very good at it sits a long way outside the box I was invited to place myself in. By the age of nine I had decided that my religion offered me very little in the way of choice. I also understood that if I wanted to follow my interest in science I might have a battle on my hands. There was one escape. Something that I could do that allowed me to be a free thinker.

I love to read and always have. Books were my treasure. I would read anything and everything. Book are a wonderful way to immerse yourself in another world, new ideas or getting a deeper understanding of something you are interested in. When I'm reading I can disappear for hours. When I was at school (it seems like only yesterday) one of the things we got every holiday was a book list. The English Department would provide about fifteen book titles for all of us to read so we could enjoy an extra opportunity to learn. The titles were mainly fiction with the occasional reference book thrown it. Some people read one or two books, quite a few read at least half of the list. I, along with a few others, read all of the list. Even the books I didn't really like somehow got digested too (My Family & Other Animals by Gerald Durrell stands out as I never really enjoyed reading about animals). I would go back to school full of books and ready for more.

As a teenager, most of my angst was confirmed by what I discovered in the pages of books. Books opened me up to other worlds, other cultures, the experiences of others. The words flowing across the page are spellbinding. If I get a book that grabs my attention, I will stay up most of the night to finish reading it. Loving science fiction I was always able to escape into future worlds. Worlds where I could have choices not currently open to me, or so it seemed. Then around the age of 17 I discovered my first spiritual book. It was called Far Memory by Joan Grant, about a past life that she recalled in Egypt. I was enthralled. I had never considered past lives as a true experience. More spiritual and religious books followed. I was searching to understand why I was here and what life was meant to be about.

I found it painful to realise that the wonder of books isn't always carried over into the 'real' world.

So, in my 20s I diverted into research - or rather, reading about research. Other people had the experiences, drew the conclusions and suggested ways I should filter my experience of the world. Think about all those diet books, DIY, cookery, travel books that are sitting on your shelf at the moment. Have you done what they write about? Best of all are the books about parenting. I had loads. But they all contradicted themselves and I gave up reading them when I found the 'one' that appealed most to me. I can't say I followed it, but I did read it!

So where is all this going? I love books but I've stepped away from them. It wasn't a painful separation as I still read. But now I read less. I came across a subject that has had so many books written about it in the last 150 years that it would be impossible to read them all. Yes, it's about being psychic or a medium. I'm sure it's not the only subject that has endless books but it's the one that made me stop and think about how much can be understood from only reading about a topic. I have read a lot in the last 15 years or so but my reading list would still only scratch the surface. I read because I wanted to understand what this phenomenon was. I read because I was sceptical. I read because the personal stories were fascinating.

I read across, around, and to the sides of the subject. The reading didn't help me truly understand what being psychic or a medium was about. But still I kept reading.

As I mentioned at the beginning of this book, eleven years ago, I had some events happening in my life that were undeniable evidence that 'something' was actively trying to connect me with the world of mediumship. Total strangers were giving me indirect messages about developing my psychic ability. It was too random to be chance. So, I found a spiritualist church and stepped inside to another world. Not necessarily a world I was totally unfamiliar with but certainly a world I had never experienced. And that is when the magic happened. In stepping into that new world - opening my mind to the possibility it might be 'real' - I found a new way of living my life. Contact with Guides can't be learned from a book. You have to be open and listening. The books I'd read (and continued to read) helped me to understand some of what was happening about the process I was engaged in, but it was the personal experiences, each random (at first) contact, each experiment to connect, each botched attempt that showed me how I connect and am able to work.

Whilst I was on this inner, spiritual journey I puzzled over the challenges to my early life beliefs. What I might once have taken for granted was slowly and steadily being turned upside down. I went back over my values and beliefs time and time again. Some changed easily and some stayed stuck for much longer. Finding that there may be an Afterlife certainly focused my attention on the way I was living. What kind of choices did I make? Could I acknowledge my 'other' self – the one that spoke with people who were missing their physical bodies? My outer world also felt the earthquakes of my changing outlook. As I discussed my experiences with family and friends they had to adjust to my new way of seeing and being. It wasn't always easy.

So what about friendships? I feel fortunate to have had many friendships in my life. Some have been for a short period or whilst I needed a different point of view. Some have lasted for many years, even though we only meet up occasionally, and feel timeless. There are many ways to define this kind of loving relationship. For me that is the key. A friendship is the connection of love you feel with someone so that you make room for them in your life as an inspirer and collaborator. You want to listen to what they say, you value their viewpoint and you feel a positive flow of energy in their company. You are prepared to overlook what you may judge to be their flaws or failings. You feel you can be relaxed and yourself with them. You feel that they will never let you down and always have your back. Of course, I'm highlighting the up side of friendship. There are times when friendships can be challenging. There are times when they can be exasperating, disappointing, broken. This is the real value of a friend. By being in our life, a friend offers us a sounding board, experiences that challenge our world view and opportunities to practice unconditional love. We collaborate in exploring the connections, boundaries and flow of loving energy between us. We drift together, apart and, sometimes, back together in a new way with new understanding. Friendship has, at its heart, giving and taking, sharing and growing.

The interesting thing for me was how some friends took a step back. Or decided to insist that I was a bit deluded. There is a psychological tactic called Gaslighting - the practice of getting you to think that your internal world isn't the real reality for you. I was interested because I have been in, on the receiving end of and probably practiced at some point in my life, coercive relationships. I'm not necessarily referring to intimate relationships. All relationships have a dynamic going on; an exchange of some kind, be it power, dependency, enabling or collaborative. It certainly didn't fit for some of my more religious friends, or the sceptical ones, that I was making contact with disincarnate beings. It was outside of the reality they understood. So, they tried very hard to dismiss my tentative steps into experiencing connections. I found myself rather strongly telling these people not to tell me my world couldn't be as I described it, or to measure and define it for me or even to say it didn't exist as a world unless they actually studied it from my side. I told them they needed to step into and experience my reality before commenting, extrapolating and second guessing how my world worked.

I was taking a stand. I was exercising my right to a reality that suited me. After all we only agree that certain things are 'givens' because we are socially conditioned to do so. I'm reminded of being the girl who was told that women were the weaker sex. That seemed to be about not being able to fight like a man, not having enough muscles or aggression. Yet the women around me seemed to have plenty of muscle power - all the heavy lifting related to looking after children, men and households - and the ability to fight like hell when their children needed to be defended. We express our social conditioning in all sorts of relationships, within our families, our occupations and our wider community. Anyone who has a different reality is identified as 'other' and is often to be feared. Then the attempts to persuade that person to share our reality begin in earnest. In the end, some people moved out of my life, some shrugged their shoulders and accepted I'd changed and some embraced my reality by stepping into it themselves.

Now I realise the value of experience. Not just because I'm in the second half of my life. I know that to try something might help me decide if I want more of it or less. Might help me to encourage others to try if they want more or less of something. That experience leads to choices. Giving people the choice to see me connect to Energy Beings through trance, or a reading or when I do a service in a church or spiritual centre can help them to decide if they want more connection or less. I'm not one for hiding aspects of my work away, for making the language or the process of experiencing spirit contact difficult.

I still think about what the final push was. The first Guide who worked with me took his time to make himself know to me. He understood that I would be testing myself every step of the way. I was reluctant to accept that there was something outside of me that could communicate but not have a physical presence. Of course, I had been a self-directed student of past lives, religion and philosophy for most of my life. I had been heavily into science fiction so open to considering that reality was not as we thought it was. My interests in astrology, dream interpretation, tarot, magic and esoteric traditions had lead me into fascinating experiences (add in the study of psychology as well). Yet I was still standing on the edge. Perhaps there were other beings who could interact with me. How would I tell them apart from all the different parts of my psyche - my human soul, mind or spirit?

So, did I fall or was I pushed. As I continued to acknowledge that I seemed to be getting information I couldn't have possible known in any other way, the sense of my Guide emerged. A personality was forming - different than my own, sometimes completely opposite from mine. Was it another aspect of me - a role I was testing out or a part of me I hadn't explored yet? The personality seemed to come with its own back story. He could recall experiences that I certainly hadn't had in this life. Was it my vivid imagination? There was a quality to these experiences, too much detail, that seemed to suggest they were 'real' memories. I admit to being intrigued. I wanted to know more, have more evidence, get more detail. My earlier objections faded away.

ABOUT SPIRIT CONNECTIONS

"When you open up to all that is around you in the energy world you find your loyal, patient and encouraging helpers and supporters. They have been waiting to talk to you all of your life. I t's worth listening to what they have to say."

Guides:

Who guides us?

How many? And what for?

The ones who aren't Guides

So what's in a name?

The Guide Contract

Meeting Wolf Running

Mum gets her say

Guides

I often get asked about my Guides. Or to tell people about their Guides. As a reluctant medium I'm also reluctant to talk about Guides in anything other than general terms. I prefer people to work out their own relationships with their Guide team because then you know what is true for you. I always talk about my Guides and Inspirers when I'm doing services, messages and teaching, and sometimes people say I inspire them to search for their guides. I'm fortunate to be working with Inspirers from the Spirit World who are recognised as positive, high vibrational beings. They help me to stay grounded as well as to work through my own knotty issues and challenges. Their encouragement, in the face of my stubbornness, is awesome. They have been patient, creative and super special at motivating me, moving me forward and nudging me along a path I might otherwise never have taken.

I love my Guides to bits. And they must certainly love me to have been so patient with me. I wasn't going to give room in my head to just anybody! So, when I started to connect with them more, they faced a barrage of questions. I was forever asking for information to be confirmed by other methods. Even detailed messages from other mediums when I was in a Spiritualist church only got a 'Maybe' in my mind. I feel that's one of the hardest parts of working with Energy Beings. Generally, it all takes place in your head so it's hard to trust the information. We have grown up in a world where science and logic have trained us to demand logical explanations for everything. So if we can't see, hear, touch, smell or taste we can be quite dismissive of our 'in the mind' experiences. I did spend quite a long time back in my world of psychology reminding myself of objective versus subjective information, experiences and mind. I'm glad I did. It all became so churned up between psychology, spirituality and spiritualism that I was completely confused. There was only one thing left to do. I had to trust that I wasn't going mad, imagining things or being a fantasist. It boiled down to trusting the experiences and thinking about the explanations later.

I have repeatedly asked why me? Especially when I've been stuck, frustrated or fed up with some aspect of our connection. It has taken me a long time to accept the answer. Because... I sometimes feel like that answer is a cop out. My Guides keep saying it will make perfect sense when I return to the Spirit World. Apparently it's all in the plan I made before I came here. I picked the life experiences I wished to have. Along with the challenges I would be tested with. It's reassuring to think there is an underlying pattern to my life but frustrating not to know it all. I guess it's another test of the trust we have in each other that I can wait for all to be revealed.

Who guides us?

It's exciting, scary and confusing when you realise that you are being contacted by Energy Beings. You want to know why they picked you. If you are not someone who believes that there are Energy Beings you are sceptical. If you have been waiting for the communication breakthrough you might be disappointed, relieved, uncertain. Guides come in all shapes, sizes, religious and experience types. They are not what you might expect. They may test your open mindedness completely. It can be hard to work with Elementals when you don't believe in fairies. So there is a big reveal occasionally. More often Guides approach you over a period of time. They go at a pace that suits them but with a real consideration for you and how far out of your comfort zone you have to move to communicate with them.

We tend to want to know the names of our Guides, their appearance, any back story about who they were in life (if they were human at any time) and why they chose us. Then we want them to hurry up and communicate faster and clearer. Finally, we often want them to have a bit of kudos. We'd quite like our Guides to be well known, to have a bit of fame, or to be seen as powerful. We fall into the trap of ranking the Guides in a hierarchy, assuming Angels are better than Spirits who are easier to relate to than gnomes or elves. A true Guide will often withhold their name until you accept working with Ms Nobody from Nowhere. They also hold back on their appearance and story for the same reason. Guides will work very hard to get your attention. They will lead you to experiences and information about connecting with them so that you start to know when and how to work with them. They will be respectful about moving you along at a pace you can handle.

Eventually they will push you into saying no. They don't need to have another sheep on their team, blindly following the orders given from 'on high'. They want to communicate with people who are not afraid to set boundaries and stick to them. They prefer that after learning to switch on you also learn to switch off. In my experience as a teacher, Guides tend to work best with reluctant mediums. Those people who challenge what their Guides suggest or ask them to do. When you finally rebel they celebrate. You have crossed over from being a passive 'instrument' into being an equal partner in an endeavour. Then the seriously fun work can start.

I've always found that a certain level of detachment has helped me to build a good and strong relationship with my Guides. Not all of them have been my cup of tea. Some of them have been polar opposite to me. Yet we have worked to understand and know one another over time. My Guides give me loving kindness. They give me support. They make sure I use my free will to choose. And they accept that I have the choice in anything I think, feel, say or do. My Guides respect me - as I respect them. If you are working to communicate, demand the same standard of contact knowing that, like any true relationship, both sides have to give and take with respect, compassion and collaboration.

How many? And what for?

First, I asked how many Guides I had. Apparently, the number is infinite. I have as many Guides helping me as I wish to allow in. That make sense to me. I never quite convinced myself that there was only one energy being guiding me. It seemed like there should be more as that is what happens on the Earth. I'd rather have lots of help than only one hard pressed, overworked Guide trying to get me to do what is in my own best interest. I also asked where all these Guides came from. It was wonderful to realise that we can be guided by many different Energy Beings so I welcomed the opportunity to work with Elementals, Aliens, Dragons, and Angels to name a few. There are many, many dimensions our Spirit is connected with so why restrict my guidance to only the human Spirit World. It's actually more important to understand what role they have than who they might be.

Firstly, we all have a Gatekeeper Guide. This Guide agrees to be with us from the moment we step out of the Spirit World until the moment we step back in. The Gatekeeper's job is to keep the lines of communication open as best s/he can so that we don't drift off what we have planned for this life. When we are travelling in a direction that is against our plan our Gatekeeper will be bouncing up and down on our head to try to get us to pay attention. When we are sailing along in accordance with our plan our Gatekeeper will be off having a cup of coffee with the other Guides, catching up with all the gossip. Most often this Guide has been with us in many past lives. We have swapped being the Gatekeeper many times for each other. That's why this Guide has the patience necessary to hang out with us until we notice that they are there. I love my Gatekeeper for being so determined to wake me up and keep me on track.

Secondly, it's often the case that family members get involved in guiding us too. After all we are more likely to trust someone in our family tree better than a complete stranger. I work with my Mum some of the time and occasionally with my Grandfather. They are a steadying force when I might have wobbles about the service

I've been asked to give. They also bring a lot of humour as they can remind me of my mistakes (or as I prefer to think of them, my prototypes), from earlier in my life, without being judgemental or picking fault. That's something we do to ourselves as we have trained ourselves to make comparisons and compete. They also understand my need to have balance in my life. If I'm doing too much they will give me a push to slow down. Or even put the brakes on for me by chasing all the rest of the team out of sight for a while.

Finally, there are the Guides who pop in for one job, one reason or one piece of development. Guides are of all energy vibrations, experiences and backgrounds. They are Energy Beings who have been around the block a bit - even the brand new ones. They are working on their development too. So, connecting with me for a 'one off' event of spiritual service can be helpful to them too. I do wonder how many of them breathe a sigh of relief when the joint task is finished. As you might have already noticed, I can be hard to convince sometimes. I like to know why I'm doing something. Not just that I have to do it. What they bring is a fresh viewpoint, a new skill or some much needed support of a different kind than my regular Guides. I don't ask their names because I don't need to know anymore. My Gatekeeper and family Guides vet these 'strangers' for me and I trust that I am sensible enough to question anyone who seems to be out of step with my vibration. I love working with my Guide team. I love working with them individually and collectively. I feel surrounded by their love and protection even when I'm at my most human and rebelling against them. I am not a robot or someone who can be led easily. They know that, respect my questions and do their best to chivvy me along the best path for me. In fact, I know they would be suspicious if I didn't question, doubt or expect answers. We have a wonderful relationship built up over many years and that's why a name has no meaning for us.

The ones who aren't Guides

As in life so with Guides. I came across Energy Beings who told me they were connecting so that they could guide me in my development or spiritual journey. Some of them seemed very plausible for a while. Until I started paying more attention to what they were asking me to do. Or how my intuition was demanding that I notice something didn't feel right. I started to listen to what they weren't saying. A counselling technique I use a lot. I noticed that these Spirits always seemed to want to feed my ego mind. Either to tell me I was the most amazing invention since sliced bread; or the worst possible medium because I only had a limited amount of talent. Distracted by the confusion their contact was causing I repeatedly asked for my Gatekeeper Guide to be the only contact I had until I could sort this out. In a way, I shut down to communicating until I could steady myself again.

In early discussions with the one guide I knew I could trust, my Gatekeeper, I found out that there are Energy Beings who are low vibrational. I don't know why I had believed that anything nonphysical must be a higher vibration but I did. Perhaps it was the combined impact of religion, judgements about myself and the influence of other 'spiritual' teachers. Maybe I was naive in thinking that the dead know better. However, just like those of us alive, there are many shades of helpfulness amongst Energy Beings. And a few who are distinctly unhelpful.

So what about the Guides who tell you they are supremely enlightened beings? Who ask you to do things that will actually cause you harm? Who suggest that pain is good for you and the world? Who ask you to use your skills to create negative energy? Who play on your ego fears? These Energy Beings aren't Guides. They really aren't. Their suggestions may look harmless at first. You may be led step by step along a path to limiting your own development without even realising what your thoughts, words and actions represent. I'm writing about this not to create fear. Communicating with Energy Beings is a wonderful experience. The point is not to let the fake Guides try to run your life. Always put any

Guide information and advice to the test. Be vigilant in passing on what they say or doing what they suggest.

So what's in a name?

As I've already said, when getting started people most often ask what the name of their Guide is. When I asked, for a long time I was told 'a rose by any other name would smell as sweet'. William Shakespeare had a lot to answer for in my eyes. Still I asked for a name. I felt somehow that if I had a name I would 'know' who my Guide was. It got much more muddled, as I exercised my psychic senses, to realise that I sensed more Guides around me. Then I started to demand names. How on earth could I build up trust, I thought, if I didn't even know who was around me. My Guides tried to encourage me to sense them rather than worry about names. Or to see or hear them instead of wanting to attach labels to their energy. I must admit I found it really, really frustrating.When I finally blew my top, they answered my anger by explaining that we were building a set of relationships. Just like in real life relationships with individual Guides take time and effort to become trusting. Would a name make the trust happen any quicker?

At this point I must have had a lightbulb moment. I recognised that I was used to being introduced to people by their name. However, I also knew that their name didn't define who they were, how they might think or feel and how they might choose to behave in any given set of circumstances. A name was only a short cut that needed to have a personality attached to it. And finding someone's personality and preferences takes time. Working with anyone over a period of time allows familiarity to develop. Predictability almost. That is what we trust. That the person we know as Annie will respond and act in given ways as certain experiences and situations arise. Hopefully Annie will respond positively - or in ways that we view as positive. If she doesn't then we might very well choose to forget we know her by forgetting her name. At this point I'm sure my Guides breathed a huge sigh of relief. I stopped asking for names. I recognised that I had to work at building a few key relationships with the Guides who were most often around me. They were my team. Working with me and supporting me to get to wherever I needed to be of service. So, I started to ask a different set of questions. Ones that have helped me understand and explain Guide teams to other people wanting to meet their Guides.

The Guide Contract

That begs the question of how you arrive at a trusting relationship that works well for both sides. Especially if, at first, you don't even know who is guiding you. I need to explain about the Contract.

When I began opening up to my Guides it seemed as if they popped in whenever they felt like it. I got woken up from sleep, grabbed when I was driving and nagged when I was doing my shopping. It took me a little while to realise that I had a say in how our relationship worked, possibly because a lot of people talk about the connection to Spirit as being a gift only a few people get. I was a little overawed to find I had this 'gift' but determined to find out more. That led me to accept the contact whenever and whoever made it. I also worried that if I refused to acknowledge the contact they would go away. That fear was really me saying I wanted to explore more, without understanding that they never go away. They only go quiet.

Eventually I got fed up of being woken up at night. I remember getting really cross and telling them to leave me alone or I would stop making contact completely. Funnily enough I started sleeping through the night again. When I got Spirit around me in everyday situations, like the supermarket or hairdressers, I started to tell them to come back when I was working at my mediumship. Finally, if I got a message when I was talking to someone in a restaurant or in the school playground I began telling the Spirits to get the person they wanted me to speak to in front of me when I was working. These boundaries created distinct spaces and reasons for how I worked my mediumship. My personal space got bigger and my mediumship time was more focused.

As I was thinking about this change one day, some time after I had put my foot down so to speak, I was sure I'd heard lots of laughter from my Guide team. Someone dropped the thought into my head that I was finally drawing up my contract. I asked what that meant. With more gentle laughter they pointed out that relationships are really contracts. They are agreements covering who does what, where, when and how. Sometimes they also specify the why. To make it work each side has to respect the expectations and responsibilities of the other. You can't do that if you haven't bothered to specify what those are. By pestering me at all times of the day and night my Guides had got me to start thinking about, and requesting, the terms of my contact with them. We were building a solid working relationship. And they pointed out that I only had to ask. Everything I had asked them to do they had delivered.

They let me process that for a few days. Then they came back and asked me what I expected and wanted from my relationship with them. They encouraged me to be specific in putting more clauses in my contract. With their prompting, I decided that I didn't want to have information that was pointless (about forthcoming events that couldn't be altered) or negative (life is always about ups and downs so why focus on the downs). I wanted my information to be uplifting for the person. If there was a tough challenge coming what could I highlight for the person to hang on to? Like any conversation, taking turns leads to clearer communication, so I asked that they speak one at a time rather than all talk to me at once. I was keen that my messages had to cause no harm, to me or to others, or I would not want to pass it on.

We also discussed the ways in which they could contact me. We agreed that I would give them a set amount of time each day during which I would be sitting quietly waiting for them to communicate. Outside of this time I would ignore their contact. The contract also included being gentle with claresentient connections as I can feel emotions and physical conditions. Having felt a heart attack as if it had been mine I was keen for this clause to be included. I was also keen to have emotional information in a way that the feelings wouldn't overwhelm me or get in the way of how I could work successfully. I wanted the content of messages to be significant for the people who I had to pass them to. I also wanted evidence to be provided. I found as I thought about this bit of the contract that I am much happier to give facts and details I couldn't possible know.

Then people can think about how I could have got that information. And I wanted these things to be confirmed by Guides more than once. I will only pay attention to suggestions or nudges from Spirit if it has been confirmed three times in three different ways. Why should it be any less for people who I pass messages on to?

During the time I was evolving my contract I was also learning about their expectations of me. They wanted me to dedicate some time to my development. It was important that when I sat down to connect I was paying attention to anything that might be a communication. Self-doubt gets in the way so much but it was my responsibility to deal with my doubts. They encouraged me to actively listen, work in a mindful manner and stay as peaceful as possible. They hoped I would share what I was getting with others so we could discuss the process of spirit communication. Finally, they expected me to question everything they said.

My Guides encourage my development through a questioning approach. They encourage me to have the experiences they arrange and to analyse them afterwards (it's part of the contract). Or more accurately to analyse my reactions to the experiences. As these things emerged in our contract I realised that I am not an instrument 'played' by my Guides, nor a vessel through which information is channelled. I am in a team and I have a say in how that team operates. Realising that rights and responsibilities cut both ways has made our working relationship very positive. I know I can renegotiate any part of my contract at any time. As a result, I love being part of the team and they never let me down.

Now our team works together to unite the two worlds by sharing understanding and knowledge with others. Often people find that meeting with their Guides is slow, tentative, frustrating. When you deepen your connection with the Energy Beings you also start to clear the past life karma that has been between you. Be patient with yourself and your Guides. There might be many very valid reasons why they are reluctant to step forward in a rush. They value the relationship you are building with them. Look for the clues they send you. I know I missed quite a few! Be open to the story behind your decision to work together. Enjoy the process of discovery. I love that I have such a devoted Gatekeeper. He loves that I am finally listening. We run with the wolves together.

Meeting Wolf Running

When I stopped worrying about what was real or imagined, about my experiences of contact with non-physical beings, I arrived at a point of peace. I decided to pay more attention to what was happening with what seemed to be my major Guide. He seemed to be a clear personality by now. I could feel his smile every time I wanted to challenge what he was telling me. Most of it was still coming in through yes/no type questions so I decided we had better speed up. That was all he needed. I started to dream about having long conversations with him. None of which I remembered in detail, just the memory of having spoken with him. Then there were the moments when I heard my name being called. Or a vivid picture would drop into my mind. Working in my development group and whenever else I could find some time, we worked my intuitive senses bit by bit. I found I had lots of questions I wanted answering. The more I found out the longer the list of questions got. It continued to get longer and longer as the connection went from modem to WiFi speed.

So, what about my first Guide? The man who waited so patiently for me to decide I wanted to get more connected with the Spirit World. He was my Gatekeeper Guide - the one who stays with you all the way through your life. From the moment you decide to fall to Earth, until the moment you are back in the Pink Perfect, this spirit will walk alongside you. The job of this particular Guide is to remind you why you came here. It's also to keep you on track. And to give you early warning when you are drifting away from your true purpose. Of course, I didn't listen to my Gatekeeper for most of my life. It's a good job he was prepared to wait. After all, he had a good reason.

Way back, when I started to explore my intuitive senses I had no idea about being a medium, nor about being in contact with Guides, or any other sort of Energy Being. I was on a search for spiritual understanding. In several meditations I found myself surrounded by wolves. There was always one beautiful, blue eyed, light coated wolf who seemed to be leading the pack. I loved the energy they brought me. As I expanded my understanding the wolves came more often. They became my protectors. They still work with me now. The wolves were my first clue. Of course, I had been working on my own past lives for years. So the next clue should have been obvious. I went along to several vision quest events and always seemed to end up with a head full of the sights and sounds of a Native American village. These experiences were very vivid. I knew very little about the traditions of the Native American nation. Yet when I went in search of information, it seemed my recall had an unexpected level of detail. Eventually I also discovered the aches and pains of that life. Literally. When you work with past lives your body 'remembers' the dis-ease in that energy life. If you seek information, your body will also show you by developing symptoms.

Still not putting the pieces together I started into developing my mediumship. At first all I could sense was as if someone was standing behind me. Sometimes I saw a large blue eye. Now and again there was a wave of warm loving energy. Over time I started to recognise a familiar feeling. It was as if I knew this energy. There was a connection. I could feel myself pulled towards this other 'person'. Then I had a sequence of dreams. In each dream I was talking to a man. In each dream he looked different. By the third dream I knew it was the same person. I remember saying 'I know it's you no matter which face you wear.' That particular sequence of dreams stopped but my 'person' started to become much stronger.

I caught glimpses of him. I asked his name. He gave me a nickname to use. I asked him why I felt so strongly connected to him. He said because. No matter what I asked about him personally he replied with jokes or no answer at all. At the same time, I found all sorts of books about Native American history kept turning up. People gave them to me as gifts, or passed them on to me after they had read them. I finally read a book called Bury My Heart At Wounded Knee. It hit home very hard. After I finished it the pains in my right knee, side and shoulder made perfect sense. They were the wounds that had killed me.

I've talked about the battle I've had between logic and intuition. My search for some sort of fixed point where I could say to my heart and my head that my experiences with the spirits were real. The struggle to step into understanding my everyday world as something magical. Although not every one can sense or accept the magic. In my research into Spiritualism I found that many mediums had Native American Guides. In fact it's become a sort of stereotypical joke. A detraction. I'd been mesmerised by the channelled teaching of Silver Birch (through the mediumship of Maurice Barbanell) and White Eagle (through the mediumship of Grace Cooke). Yet many people dismissed Native American guides as the 'must have' accessory for any 'fake' medium. So, although I received the information about a Native American past life (two actually) and connections to a guide who was Native American I still resisted what I was learning.

I had to decide what I wanted to do. And deal with the fear that I was fooling myself. Had my mind built a fantasy out of a desire to somehow feel more special or important? It's a difficult question. One that trips up more good mediums than not. I know a number of people who have placed their mediumship development on hold because they are uncertain about having a Native American guide. Examining the resistance took me on quite a journey. It was a real test of belief and trust. Was I falling in with the suggestion from Christine, so long ago now, that she could see a Native American man standing beside me wanting to talk? Had I somehow been influenced by my reading to feel I needed that kind of guide so I had credibility? Was I really connected to those past lives, or this person, as I felt I had been? Could I trust my recall against the possibility that I'd read all these things in books? Or seen them on the TV? So many questions chasing my sceptical mind around and around. I remember I worked myself into so much doubt that I kept insisting that everything had to be backed up. Prove it to me, I kept saying.

Amazingly, or not so when you understand the Guides, even random strangers were involved in passing on confirmations.

Several conversations suddenly shifted into talking about Native Americans or their traditions. My friend gave me a pack of medicine wheel oracle cards out of the blue. I was given an ornament – the head and shoulders statue of a Native American chief. All sorts of little hints and tips. Then a picture of a Native American warrior arrived when I was at Mind, Body, Spirit Fair. Drawn to the picture my friend bought it for me. In a short period of time I also received a card with a wolf on it. A box of cards I bought turned out to be pictures of wolves. My friend asked me about the book Women Who Run With The Wolves. It's a book I treasure so I began to understand that all of these threads were the ways in which my Gatekeeper Guide wanted to prove himself to me.

It took me a little while longer to work through all of the final bits of resistance I had been carrying. I know it's often hard for us to accept the level of unconditional love that our Guides represent. Human love is so very conditional. Even when we think it isn't, it still is. I had to be able to love myself enough to accept that my Guides wanted to work with me. That they would do so with or without names and back stories. And that if I had 'run mad' it was a glorious madness waiting to be embraced and explored. I knew it was time to fully embrace this madness. I made the decision to step off the cliff into a different way of being knowing that I wouldn't turn back. Possibly that I couldn't turn back. Yet what was being offered gave me the chance to experience a completely different way of life. Something better. Something more me.

A few nights after that I lay in bed talking to my Gatekeeper. I told him I knew where we had been together last. The image of that final battle was strong in my mind. I also knew that he had not intended me to die. His love for me was so strong that he had carried a sense of guilt and blame back into the Spirit World. That was a part of his karmic consequences. His decision to stay there and help me from that side of life was all about protecting me better. He had made his presence known so slowly because he thought I would reject him. In those moments I understood why he had been testing me. He wanted to make sure that I could accept him and work with him. As we spoke and I released him from the promise he had made himself he told me his true name. That is when Wolf Running took his place fully beside me.

Mum gets her say

Previously I mentioned our family guides. One day, not so long after I started my public work, I found out that my Mum, Ellen, worked with me. It was quite a shock when my Mum stepped in. We had a loving but challenging relationship when she was alive. I come from a line of independently minded women. Our family history is the stuff of a romantic novel. Only, the reality of what makes a good Catherine Cookson story is hard to actually live. My Grandmother lost her Mum when she was a toddler. My Mum lost her Dad when she was seven. They were both placed in a position where self-reliance was a key survival trait. They had it in bucket loads. Being around them, especially with a rebel in my head, it's no surprise that I wanted to do things my way and for myself. Alongside that was the pressure of being an eldest child.

Three small children is a handful for anyone. My Mum had different expectations for me than my brothers. I'm sure it was because at seven, as the eldest, she stepped into a lot more responsibility for her siblings. Her father died. Leaving his wife and four children in a harsh world having to fend for themselves. Mum's youngest brother was only six weeks old. My widowed grandmother, Elsie, had to go back to work and the children were farmed out to other relatives for some of the time. In a way, my Mum became the one to look after the others. So she expected me to be much more of a help with my brothers than perhaps would have been the case in another family. It was as if, because she had to, I would automatically have to too. But I wanted my freedom. Being responsible didn't fit with freedom. So we clashed. In fact, clashing became part of our relationship. If she wanted me to do something she would tell me to do the opposite knowing full well I would rush off and do what she had really wanted all along. She used to tell me when I was older that every adult should be able to be one step ahead of their child. Mum felt it was very much a part of the responsibility the adult took on for their child. In my teenage years, when I got wise to that tactic, I'm sure I was much more of a trial to her.

Mum was big on responsibility and duty. She was bright too. Yet she chose to work to help support the family household. There was no money to send her to university. She had a sister and brothers who needed to be fed. She left school after her exams to work in the mill office where my Nanna worked. Having experienced the juggling of tight budgets, having a slate at the corner shop and days where meals were meagre, she knew her wage was valuable. It's interesting to me that she never spoke about her Dad. Or how it felt to lose him. The change in her life was enormous but it was not up for discussion. In fact, for most of my childhood I was unaware that my Granddad was actually my step granddad. When I asked her about it later in my life I got a few bald facts. Nothing else. Now I know that her grief was still locked up inside. It was a place she couldn't visit. I know that her Dad came for her when she passed but it must have been difficult for her to contain all her grief for so long. I'm sure that is a big part of why her emotions stayed well under control most of the time. When I was in the drama of feelings, she was cool and detached. We spoke of love very infrequently. Her past seemed to make her lose her ability to hug or be physical with people. Apart from the occasional goodnight kiss she remained remote.

But she could be very funny. When she laughed you felt included in that warmth. Perhaps from her point of view there was very little in life to laugh at. What she placed her trust in was her religion. She was very involved in and loyal to our local church. Even after we moved we used to go back to our 'own' church every Sunday. She did charitable work in the church, cleaning and fundraising. As we grew up and flew the nest it became her life. Her marriage hadn't brought her what she expected either. My Dad loved her to bits, but I guess he couldn't fill the gap she felt. He also had his own issues to deal with. He worked hard and stressed about money. However, he transferred his stress to Mum and their relationship was sometimes very stormy. In the end, I think he felt he had lost her somewhere throughout the years. And she felt that the love she had given up everything for hadn't delivered the life she dreamed of. Like most people of their generation they rubbed along somehow. Dad was devastated when she died. After more than 45 years his anchor had gone. That was Mum's skill. Somehow, she anchored us all. She helped us do the right thing as she saw it. She chivvied us along, wanted the best for us and pushed us to get it for ourselves.

Quite a challenge then for us to work together as medium and Guide. Lots of family history and karma from past lives to clear. A different relationship was definitely required; not the least because I was still angry that she had left Dad on his own. Angry with myself. Where had the time gone? Why hadn't I been there for her more? Anger with my Mum for going when I had a two and a half year old daughter. Anger that I didn't have her guidance about how to be a parent. So many angry feelings about the hospital. Angry at my Dad and brother who knew she was fading away but didn't tell anyone. That is where I got stuck in my grief about her passing. Until I could get past the anger, how would we be able to trust one another. I've already said I must have been a challenge to my Guides. Learning that my Mum was one of them was their challenge back to me.

It started with a dream. About six months after she died, my Mum came into my dream. She wanted to show me why she had to go and what she was doing now. I went with her to a house where she was looking after a disabled child. I wasn't surprised as my Mum loved children. She had her happiest moments sharing the innocence of childhood with every small child she came across. A part of her was always the curious seven year old in that time before her Dad died. She slipped back there very easily when she was around young ones. Finding out that she was around a young boy helping him have a good life was a wonderful revelation. I recall sitting at a kitchen table with her. She asked me what was bothering me still. I was able to tell her that I was angry at the way she left Dad. She said she knew but she had no choice. Other duties were calling her and she explained that I would understand one day. As I came out of the dream I felt as if a little of the anger had somehow slipped away.

Trying to find a way to deal with my grief became a focus of my spiritual search. As a counsellor I could, of course, recognise and describe the grieving process. It's a lot easier to be the observer rather than the experiencer. I can't say I was thinking exactly straight either. I feel the anger got in the way of things a lot. I plodded on through the ups and downs of being a fairly new mum feeling like I had lost my main anchor. Who could I ask when I needed to deal with things that affected my daughter? Who was going to support and encourage me that I could be a good mum too? Even if she didn't agree with my choices. Once again, I was looking outward to deal with inner turmoil. At the same time, all of these emotions seemed to connect me deeper into my intuition. I used my Tarot cards all the time trying to get a message from Mum. I went to one or two events hoping that Mum would give the medium a message for me. I wanted the connection. The reassurance that she was really there, ok and happy. I also needed to hear from her for me. I wanted my anchor back. In the end, that urge, along with all of the things that were happening to me when I was trying to communicate, got me into the spiritualist church.

The first time I walked into Colne Spiritualist church I felt a sense of coming home. Colin, the man I had spoken to on the phone was playing a tune I knew as The Old Rugged Cross. He wouldn't have known but we played that song at both my Nanna's and my Mum's funerals. It was the perfect confirmation for my new journey into the psychic side of life. I waited and waited for month after month to see if my Mum would bring me a message. She never did. My Grandfather Jack came along several times. Even Gladys, the lady who trained me in my first job, put in an appearance. But not Mum. After a long wait I lost patience. I started asking her to show herself and give me a message. My Guide team must have been very happy when I made those requests. They were ready to spring another surprise. Of course, they had already got me up on my feet giving messages. I was doing church services. One evening I felt like Wolf Running had stepped back. Just as I was going to do my service. Where was my Guide? Who was going to help with the connections? A picture of my Mum popped into my head. I thought she was there to represent that I would be giving someone a message from their mum. That's what I stood up and did.

For the rest of the service, and for quite a few afterwards, I would get the picture of my Mum in my mind just before I started. The first message would be from someone's mum and I would feel like I was working without any Guides involved. I kept asking what was going on. Then at one service I saw my Mum marshalling a queue of spirit people. She was getting them in line and telling them what order to step forward. I had a brief chance to ask her what she was doing and she said she was there to organise me. On the way home I asked lots of questions of my Guide team. Could my Mum really be working with me? Why? How? All sorts of thoughts bounced around my mind. My delight at her presence was tinged with the grief of missing her. When I got home I sat in my meditation chair and told them to explain themselves fully. Mum stepped in immediately. I saw her in my mind's eye but, more clearly, felt her standing beside me. It was time for us to work out a new way of relating. And a new way for me to work with my Guide team.

Mum has been working with me for the last nine years. She came because I could trust her. She knew I would recognise her energy signal any where, any when. She is not allowed to interfere with my free will – none of the Energy Beings are – so she rarely offers any comment about what I'm doing with my daughter, my work or my life. However, she does help me to work with the Spirit People when I am doing services or readings. She knows that I feel it's a privilege to communicate on behalf of Spirits so she keeps my visitors organised and to the point. She also lets me know when I can trust the information or energy I'm getting. She isn't fooled easily so will bounce away time wasting people and spirits. Mum is also a great help if the energy vibration is a bit flat. She dances around in my head, or gets jokey, so that I feel like giggling. She soon gets the bubble and sparkle back. Mum especially enjoys it when my Spirit children guides come to play too. There is a special area where the children live, surrounded by loving helpers, so they can wait for their family members to meet them when they too have passed over. If they want to, the children can help with guiding us, sharing their playfulness and excitement. Spirit children love to bring in a happy vibration because it makes connecting with the Spirit World much easier. We have a lot of fun on paranormal investigations with the children. I know that we are resolving our past and present life karma by sharing the work for Spirit. Recently she has stepped back so she can work with my daughter. I'm delighted to let her go as it's time for her to be a Grandma now. I'm looking forward to keeping in touch with her until the time we will be reunited in the Pink Perfect.

WORKING WITH ENERGY

"There is a whole new world waiting to be discovered. If you are curious, adventurous and willing to explore your inner self. There is work to be done to improve your life, your tribe and your world. Each one can reach one and teach one. The love will spread. All you have to do is take the first step."

Kick starting the healing

All the Clares

Doubt does creep in – for all the right reasons

Improving the connection

Evidence that brings the inner certainty

Working for Spirit in public

Why do I do it?

Afterlife is Life

Boundaries

Kick Starting the Healing

Working with my Guides I quickly learned that my aura was a muddy mess. So that they could get through to me, I first had to be paying attention to their contact. I also needed a positive energy path for them to pass through and into my aura. Energy Beings connect their aura energy to ours in this way. If my aura is full of old, stuck, stagnant and low level energy, there is no bridge into my intuitive senses for a Guide to use. This was part of the wisdom I was busy learning. My Guides also encouraged me to tackle the stuck stuff. If I could release old feelings and thoughts my energy would be lighter. I could be more effective in my mediumship. And best of all, I would understand how to help other people who were making their own healing journeys.

They were so keen for me to begin that as soon as I started attending the Spiritualist church they had my neighbour, a Reiki Master, approach me one day. She was slightly apologetic but determined in her mission. My Guides had contacted her healing Guides to ask if she would approach me to suggest I do my Reiki Level 1 training. She was slightly uncomfortable because she tended to ignore the connection to Spirit Guides so this was a first for her. I considered for about a second and said yes. After all, if my Guides had gone to all that effort it must be important.

Having completed my Reiki attunement I took the opportunity to have Spirit Healing at the church. I was interested to see if there was any difference between the two types of energy work. I know people who will disagree but I found that there was no perceptible difference. In both situations I experienced the same sort of reactions. I also felt a warm, glowing sense of love. It seemed that I had been having this energy on lots of other occasions too. It was familiar and comforting. The more I used my switched-on healing hands, the more I seemed to bring in increased amounts of energy. When I asked my newly discovered healing Guide what was happening, he explained that my own self-healing ability, the wise part of my consciousness that wanted me to be well and in balance, had kicked in. I was amazed. It seemed I had always been able to be physically, mentally, emotionally and spiritually well. Of course, I'd read about this subject over quite a few years but the sceptic in me denied it was possible. Even, as a counsellor, knowing all that I did about the power of the mind, I struggled to be a believer in self-healing. There seemed to be a lack of definitive scientific evidence to back it up. My healing Guide explained that I had a lot to do. As well as lightening my aura I would need to heal my past life issues and release as much baggage as I could. I would also have to open my mind further about the nature of self-healing.

Where to start? And why? The why was easy. I wanted to connect better with the Energy Beings. The where was a little more of a puzzle. I had already looked at a few of my past lives to see what patterns they brought into my present life. Should I look at my physical health and would it involve exercise? The tomboy had stopped being active a long time ago. What about more counselling? I'd had a couple of periods of the talking therapy already. Did I need more? My Guides were distinctly firm. The place to start was with clearing up the energy in my aura. I have to say it took me quite a long time of practicing aura cleansing to feel that the connection was getting better. My Guides assured me that all the cleaning and polishing I was doing to my aura would make a big difference in tuning in to them. They encouraged me to stick at it, be organised and to keep looking for the positives.

So what was I doing? As well as setting the intention, every time I had a shower, to 'wash' my aura as well as my physical body I started to look at what feelings or thoughts I might still be holding on to. Holding onto feelings or thoughts often pulls our energy to focus on the very thing we are trying to let go of. I certainly felt that I kept dragging my past into my present day. To clear those issues, I started to explore why I might still have thoughts or feelings about past experiences. Especially where the feelings or thoughts were full of low vibrational energy e.g. anger, sadness, depression, guilt, envy, to name a few. Then I started to accept that what I was feeling or thinking was okay for that moment in time but not necessarily for now. I saw how the old feelings and thoughts were holding me back so I imagined them fading slowly away bit by bit every day. It's surprising how easy it is to clean old energies away if you tackle the task in small steps.

Another way to clean and clear my aura was to use affirmations. One of our greatest gifts is our ability to think and to have a choice in what we think about. Sometimes we tell ourselves we can't change our thinking but there is ample evidence that we can - if we really want to. Using positive words in our thinking builds the feeling of positivity within us. That's why we respond to praise and recognition. It's how to build self-confidence in ourselves and each other. Often written about as a Positive Mental Attitude, this way of rephrasing the language we use in our heads is also helped by using positive affirmations. If I find I'm focusing on my worries I swap the worry thoughts for encouraging words. One of my favourite mantras is 'You can do anything you choose to'. I also like to use 'Today is a brilliant day'. It might take some time for the phrase to oust the worry thoughts but by repeating it I know I am moving into a more positive frame of mind. Acknowledging the doubt behind the worry also lets me find the fear. Fear is at the bottom of all of the excuses we give ourselves not to do something. It is the way we justify staying safe within our comfort zone.

However, if we really want to accomplish something in our lives, we have to work past the fear, doubt and worry. To shine, we must polish ourselves. I remember all of one week going around muttering under my breath 'you are a ray of sunshine' just so I could prove to myself that affirmations work. My muttering made me smile. It was amazing how many other people smiled back. By the end of the week I'd stopped muttering as the phrase had gone inside my head. I had started to believe that I was shining through my days. Using positive statements helped me deal with the belief that I was lazy, that I was never on time and that giving to others was more important than giving to myself. All those beliefs had created stuck energy, powerful emotions and unreal thoughts. No wonder my aura was muddy.

The best part of all the cleansing work I was doing was to really experience consistent communication with my Guides. As my aura got cleaner, my personal vibration lifted to be more positive and they could connect with me so much better. Then the real work could begin. My mediumship has been steadily improving ever since I created the space in my aura. Now I treat myself to an aura Spring clean as often as I can. The work of cleansing doesn't really end. It's surprising what stray, random energies you can collect as you wander around in the world. Not to mention the experiences that can still produce a wobble. Every time I become emotional, or my thoughts refuse to be calm, I know I have uncovered another patch to clean, clear and shine. Getting that patch of aura energy sorted means more positive energy flowing through and around me. If I'm more positive then I can shine more energy out to others and that is the best of all reasons to clear, clean and polish like never before.

Alongside all the aura work my Guides sent me other signals, pointers to where something was limiting my intuitive ability. They had picked up on my ability to practice lucid dreaming which I have done for many years. This is when the dreamer is aware that they are in a dream state and can take control of the dream to understand it better or even to stop the dream in its tracks. So, I try to notice my dreams. It's often another way for the Energy Beings to communicate with us or for our own Higher Self to bring information into our conscious mind. Vivid dreams that stay with us (at least for a few moments after we wake) are worth writing down as often they are part of a sequence. Recording as much as I can about them and looking for patterns helps me work out things that are blocking me, my communication or point out other issues I need to pay attention to. It might sound a bit odd to say that but dreams usually flow from one sequence to another. The imagery fits together in some creative, abstract way but it does make sense on some level. Thinking about the way I approach dream interpretation - examining each layer of the dream and its symbols - I can often uncover an old thought or feeling. Or a belief about myself that is no longer true – if it ever was. Then it's time to remind myself that energy flows. Only our physical body is almost static, fixed energy. In the flow of energy we can also pick up on a leading edge of the next energy wave. We can tune in to the information from the wave that relates to ourselves. The dreams help us get ready for the wave of emotion that is due to hit next. In its jumbled up pattern it is trying to give us a predictive message; a way around blocks, obstacles and limitations. Recognising where I am holding myself back and how I could move forward, I noticed that I was less likely to collect stuck feelings or thoughts. Noticing my dreams is also a powerful way to heal myself.

Over time I felt I needed to do my Reiki 2 and Master/Teacher attunements. These would open up more energy levels to help my healing journey. The final one would help me deal with my spiritual uncertainty. To take these steps I knew I needed to give myself more time and space. I was offering healing energy to others so that they could kick start their own healing process. Each person I channelled the energy to helped me to reflect on my road to wellbeing. Reflecting. Thinking about what just happened. Processing my life's experiences. I needed silence. I realised that one of the things I love is being able to find some silence. It's precious, golden, priceless to have moments with no outer distractions. It's an opportunity to step off the planet for a while. I let the silence envelop me and listen to my mind running on about all the everyday concerns. It's not quite like a meditation, I'm not trying to still my thoughts. Actually I want to listen to them; to see what themes are going around and round in my head. It's a way to let the worry and fear surface from the corners I've pushed them into so I can find out how I might be holding on to stuck stuff.

I'm very good at keeping going. It's one of my most impressive abilities. I can persevere in the face of many of life's challenges. I focus on getting through. I'm stoical. (Thank you for that skill, Mum.) However, when I am out the other side of the challenge, I often think that I still have to keep going, putting on a brave face and being strong. Letting silence surround me, so that thoughts and feelings about what has happened can emerge, can be the last thing I want to do. Or to let my thoughts about any future concerns come to the front of my mind. Most of us have been socialised to worry about the future. We plan for it, save for it and have expectations about it. It takes our attention from the here and now. In the background of our everyday thoughts, there are strands of ideas all about the future and how we wish it will be. Getting to that future seems fraught with more challenges so we worry or are fearful that we will miss out on what we are hoping for.

When I sit quietly in the golden silence, I notice all of these strands bouncing around my mind. I have the opportunity to check if any of the worries or fears are actually real. I also have a chance to see if they are tied into my past experiences in case I am dragging my fears forward with me. It's also the time when I notice other feelings and thoughts. Ones that seem to belong to someone else or more than one person. Letting the precious silence in gives me a chance to listen both to my Higher Self - my Spirit - and to my Guides. What I 'hear' is inspiration, encouragement, creative solutions and practical suggestions. There is a lot of comfort gained in letting other voices speak inside my mind. It's also an activity that keeps me firmly in the now. Silence supports mindful practice because there are no outer distractions to remove your attention from the inner experience.

As I carried out my service to the Spirit World and the people left behind down here, using the silence to continue my own healing journey became very important. The spiritual journey is always first an inward one. We have to find out and understand who and what we are before we can offer ourselves back to the world to be of service. And being of service to ourselves and others is at the heart of practicing spirituality rather than simply talking about how spiritual we are. If I honour the silence by paying attention in it, I will be ready to turn to the outer world much sooner. For me, silence is a gift. It is the most valuable time I can spend because I am spending it on and with myself. It is a space where my inner Light can increase because I am paying attention to truly knowing myself. There is the true meaning of healing that my Guides wanted me to understand. My authentic self is a beautiful, bright, unique Light and it is time for me to let myself shine.

All the Clares

A question I'm often asked is how I connect with my Guides or the Spirit people. I believe we all have six psychic senses - to feel, see, hear, smell, taste or know energy information. These are the ways we get information from Energy Beings.
I also believe that we have to understand that we are also energy beings rather than human beings when getting the connection going at the right speed to make sense of the information. The more we make sense of what we get, the more confident we feel. As we get more confident, connecting becomes easier and we can actually speed up our development process. So, it doesn't, in the end, matter which way we perceive the energy information through our intuitive psychic senses. What really matters is being able to process it faster.

It's always worth knowing what the intuitive psychic senses are. Here are my definitions – the ones that make sense to me. They are present in everyone and I use all of them in my mediumship. I'm going to start with the one that I know best. My first experiences came through my ability to sense or feel the physical or emotional presence of non-physical people. It's called claresentience – meaning clear feeling – and covers a wide range of sensations including taking on the emotional mood of the Spirit you are connecting with. The next one I really recognised in my self was clarecognisense – meaning clear thoughts or knowing – when ideas, thoughts or lightbulb moments pop into mind with no apparent connection with what is being thought in that moment. I have to say it was hard for me to sort this intuitive sense out; between what was my thought and what was being placed in my mind by another presence. The best I can explain is that I have a sense of certainty when I'm getting clear knowing thoughts. I don't know why I know but I do know that if I verbalise those thoughts they will be correct for whoever is listening. I use clarealliance – clear smell – quite a bit now as I work with channelling the fragrances from the Angelic Realm. It ties in rather well with my claregustibus – clear taste – if it's important for a communicator to share information about their likes and dislikes as evidence for their loved ones. My intuitive hearing has come a long way since the first few words I was finally able to hear. Clareaudiance – clear hearing – allows me to work on a voice vibration so I can often pick up accents or characteristics of a person's way of speaking. Finally, there is clarevoyance – clear seeing. People often think this is the only way to get information because we are such a visual people. We rely on sight far more than any of the other senses. Actually, mediumship involves all of these senses. I remember all of my struggles in my first development group to 'see' what everyone else was seeing. I was very frustrated to find I couldn't get any information by seeing. However, as soon as I switched my attention to my other senses, in a very short time the flow of information became overwhelming.

For anyone setting off on a similar journey the starting point is to work out which way you process the energy information. Are you strongest at seeing, hearing, sensing? Or there might be two or three ways you can 'translate' the energy information. Your Guides will have been trying to point you in the right direction most of your life. We often dismiss the gut or instinct feelings we have about things because we have learned to doubt the information. Perhaps it doesn't always come in clear and understandable. Sometimes the speed that the information flows is too slow or too fast. Sometimes our rational brain tells us it can't be correct. Lots of things get in the way so we wander along wondering if there is anyone there. All around us there are signs to tell us to pay attention to the intuitions but it's easier at times to ignore them.

The question that gets asked next, when someone realises that they can sense things without knowing how they are doing it, is 'How do I develop it?' Finding out that you have intuition, that you know stuff without being told, and that you are accurate about what you sense can be confusing. We are told that psychic, or intuitive, senses don't exist, or they are a special gift, or that they are possibly a mental health issue. A good first step is always to be open minded about what is happening. Notice how often you 'guess' things right, how you are tuning in to other people's feelings or seem to know their thoughts, or always seem to end up meeting the right people at the right time. Then set aside some time to work at developing your abllily. I suggoct to my students that they sit quietly two or three times a week and ask in their thoughts for information to be given to them. I also recommend that they keep a notebook handy and write down what they feel, hear, see or think. It takes time to see if a pattern emerges and to understand the way Guides will be building the relationship.

Less discussed in development, is that our intuitive psychic senses also process the energy from the people physically around us as well as the Spirits who are no longer physical presences. As we start to recognise the energy of other people by paying attention to the information our intuitive senses bring in, we might also become aware of the emotions of our family and friends. I feel we are more comfortable recognising emotional information that we pick up from others. Sometimes we feel that a friend is sad, or a colleague is angry or a family member is in a low mood. We are often prompted by that to ask how how they are feeling. Or do something spontaneous to help them feel better. When we care about someone the energy link is strong so it is perfectly sensible that we get a bigger 'hit' of anything that might be affecting them. Sorting out the information from physical and non-physical beings is the point at which we often give up. I know that I got completely tied up in knots trying to sort out if what I was experiencing was the product of my mind, the energy of the people around me or a communication from a non-physical being. I got tangled up for quite a while. I began to doubt everything I was experiencing.

Doubt does creep in – for the right reasons

Rather in despair, I asked lots more questions. I guess I didn't just ask… I demanded answers. I doubted that I had any intuitive senses in the first place. And because I doubted that I would be able to pick up any information through my intuitive senses, I doubted the information assuming it wouldn't be correct. Finally, once it seemed that what I was getting was correct, incredibly correct, I doubted that I would be able to do anything with my ability to connect. A lot of people see doubt as a negative quality. We are often told to have faith as if we can automatically stop asking questions and believe everything we are told.

I love that I have had that period of doubt. I've asked questions all my life. Whatever has been presented to me as the 'truth', the facts or the only thing to believe, I have wanted to ask 'who says that this is so?' I have also doubted myself. Evolving my understanding of who and what I am as a spirit in a human body has often been through challenging the way I understand myself. Of course, my doubts have let me say I can't do this or that. Certainly I have passed up opportunities because I thought I couldn't do something. Or that I wasn't the one who should be doing it. Yet amazingly, after all the doubts, questions and self-challenging, I have moved my understanding of myself and humanity forward. Out of the doubt has come certainty about my values and beliefs.

I love to share my experiences. Anyone who knows me will say I can talk forever. I always encourage people to question what I tell them. My world view may not be your world view. That is refreshing. It's wonderful to discuss different points of view. Discussing, questioning, swapping experiences is a way for me to hear out loud my own doubts or questions. Also, to hear my own opinions and sticking points. Voicing doubt is a way to help me consider if I'm doing the right thing for me. We love patterns. Humans generally prefer to live by routines. In fact, in groups if someone is out of step with the routine there will be subtle (and sometimes not so subtle) pressure on that person to conform with the group. What happens if that pattern only suits some or a few of the group? How do we change the pattern if no one voices any doubt?

When I finally decided to investigate my intuitive senses, I stepped outside of my pattern. I was somewhat out of step with my group. Mediumship is still a stereotype for the table tapping, crystal ball gazing, 'is there anyone there?' lady of a certain age with loads of cats and jingling bracelets. Ok, I am a certain age and I have two cats. No jingling bracelets though! The doubts I experienced were a powerful energy to move me forward in search of other patterns and new groups. I widened my horizons, stepped away from the conventional view of mediums and psychics and started to discover a whole new life. My doubt drove that journey. My questions were answered one by one and have led to more questions. I have faith in my connection to the Energy Beings I work with. It is a faith that has emerged through the test of doubt. A faith that is stronger because I doubted. In my opinion, doubt is a fascinating road to travel.

Improving the connection

Getting a connection going, coping with the doubt and fears, persevering. That's a great start. But what next? I'm often asked how someone can improve their connection to the Spirit World. When I say 'wardrobe disaster' they often look blank. It makes no sense. What has a wardrobe disaster got to do with the Spirits of our loved ones? I had the same blank look when I asked my Guides to help me get more accuracy in my messages and evidence. There was a lot of gentle laughter and a delicate pulling together of several threads of knowledge I already had stored away in my mind. Let me explain what they told me.

Part of our human identity tends to be the clothes we wear, the 'look' we adopt and the fashion we follow. Clothes act as a visual short-cut to who we are. We present our style to the world as the outward reflection of our inner self. We also use clothing styles as a stereotyping short cut - goth, designer, hippie, rocker, sporty to name but a few. Our clothes also allow us to blend in with whoever we decide is our tribe. They bring a sense of belonging and security, or of wishing to be something when we don't think we really are. They can give clues to our ambitions, our state of mind, our values and our judgements. We all look at what the person is wearing and decide whether they 'belong' or not.

If, like me, you have been searching the whole of your life for an identity, tribe or particular values, your wardrobe might still contain lots of clothing that you have symbolically outgrown. I even have one of my baby dresses carefully put away with my first baby shoes. There have been many outfits that didn't fit, were restricting, were only a fad or wore out quickly. I've worn the strangest combinations, colours that did nothing for me and items either scratchy and uncomfortable, or so ill-fitting that I got exasperated. In other words, plenty of disasters. Yet I hang on to some of these items because they are still really new, might come in one day or represent memories.

My wardrobe contains a lot of baggage. It's suggested that

anything you haven't worn for six months should be donated to charity or thrown away. Why do I find that so difficult? I admit to resisting a great big wardrobe clear out. The clothes do represent aspects of me - the bits I decided not to be. There might bo time to try those 'outfits' still. My Guides love my determination to keep my wardrobe full to bursting. But they also explain that hanging on to old energy - represented by the clothes - makes it hard for new energy to come in. How will I be able to get space for my new look if I don't clear out the old stuff? Especially since what I'm hanging on to could be classed as 'disasters' - parts of me I really don't want to be again (suits with large padded shoulders springs to mind) or that I've worn much too often (I'm thinking of my liking for faded jeans for all occasions, weddings and funerals included).

They use the discussion about a wardrobe to help me understand that my aura is full of energy (and not only the energy obtained in this life). Every single moment of my life is captured in the way the energy flows or sticks in my aura. So, there are lots of patches of free flowing energy alongside patches that have become static. Where the energy flows freely the Spirit people, who are also energy, can connect with me and transfer information to me. My intuition and conscious mind can translate that information into a conversation, messages or evidence from the Spirit. The fixed energy is like a barrier. It gets in the way of the information coming through. It stops me translating the Spirit energy into something useful. Like a wardrobe packed too tight with old clothes, there is no room to squash the new ones in. The stuck patches are where I have held onto an experience, perhaps been hurt by it, or angry with it or fearful of what I've encountered. Those fixed blocks represent sadness, disappointment, rejection, hate, lack, loneliness and so much more. They are the clothes that don't fit, are uncomfortable or the wrong style and colour.

If I want to communicate more clearly, I have to deal with the stuck energy. So, with their gentle encouragement, I started to take the 'clothes' out of my wardrobe. Some had to be put back as I wasn't ready to let them go. Many were released to be used elsewhere. I found I had space. Room to change and grow. New outfits to try on and buy. Bit by bit, my baggage has disappeared. It's not all gone. There are still outfits I'm holding on to and some of them also relate to my past lives. I'm comfortable that when the right moment comes I will let those clothes go too. I'm also open to trying on new clothes because I know I have all the space I need to accommodate them. I have turned a wardrobe disaster into wardrobe freedom.

Turning aura disaster into aura freedom is possible if you start by acknowledging that you have been hanging on to past experiences too tightly. Exploring why you are resisting the letting go process is a key part of understanding the deeper meaning that the experiences have had. Often you will find that the experiences represent judgements you have made (or taken on board) about yourself. The stuck energy can become like a mask you wear to keep yourself safe from similar experiences. Removing the mask is a brave act. You are freeing up space to allow yourself to grow. It may seem that there is no benefit from freeing up space. That it's all rather challenging. Yet what you gain is the increased connection with Energy Beings. The loving presence of your Guides and Inspirers.

Evidence that brings an inner certainty

All the doubt and the clearing helped me to deal with one of the biggest challenges of living in my intuitive world. Many people criticise mediums for cold reading or clever guessing. It is difficult to manage a message if someone is giving you too much of their personal information rather than letting you tell them what you are getting. However, real mediums work hard not to ask questions, to only take yes or no answers and to ignore any body language. We prefer to get the evidence direct from Spirit. And we look for evidence that is more out of the ordinary too.

It's important here to make a distinction between the contact with Spirit beings and with the people who are around in the physical world. As I explained earlier, we can also get information from the aura energy of people around us. When you are able, like me, to 'read' someone's aura energy, there is always the possibility that the information you might get is coming from the energy they are giving off. This is definitely not a Spirit connection. It's the connection all of us can use intuitively. So, someone working towards excellence in their mediumship will take great care to close the intuitive human to human connection before opening the Spirit to medium connection. And will look for information from the Spirit that is of a different quality to what could be 'read' about the person in front of them.

That is what is exciting about developing your own intuitive connections. If you wish to move on to connecting with the Spirit World your Guides will show you ways of working more and more accurately. They want the same excellence so that the people getting messages feel the love and support of their loved ones even if we are temporarily in two different worlds. It's about aiming high. The sky really is the limit. The more you ask for evidence the clearer it will come through. I have to say that I'm very lucky. I have had a passion (some would probably say an obsession, lol) for excellence all my adult life. When I found I was making connections to Energy Beings I decided that I wanted good quality, clear and precise evidence. That way, I could be sure that I was connecting to a Spirit, that the message following the evidence was clear and helpful and that I was doing the best I was capable of. Evidence certainly served me well when I took my next step. Going public!

Working for Spirit in public

I freely confess to having been a sceptic, perhaps even a non-believer, in anything of the Spirit. I love science, logic and theories of how things work. Being curious led me to observe effects that I was experiencing, that eventually led me to uncover my own intuitive and Spirit connections. To say that the journey reshaped my beliefs is probably an understatement. It took me 12 years to acknowledge that things were happening to me and around me that had no logical explanation. When I finally stepped into a Spiritualist church in 2005, I was fascinated to discover that there were explanations for all the experiences I was having. Not always clear explanations nor always logical. But explanations. I decided to jump into this intuitive world and experience it before dismissing it. I was sure it would end up being dismissed as not real. Certain, in fact! Yet here I am 11 years later - convinced by my own experiences and evidence that what happens is a real thing. And standing up in front of people sharing my connection with the world of Spirit.

Over the last 11 years I have read, researched and questioned what I do as much as I possibly can. Many people will tell you I'm no pushover. I don't change my mind easily either. I reflect on what I do, am told and experience. I believe that the best way to work to raise awareness that the Spirit world may be there is to give evidence, pass on messages and be in as many places as possible sharing my world view. I don't seek to 'convert' anyone but I do expect respect for my views just as I respect anyone else's right not to agree with my views. It's a position I arrived at based on my own journey. After all, I had been giving messages publicly for three years before I was ready to agree that there was enough evidence for me to say that the World of Spirit was as real as this one. Thank goodness the Spirits kept turning up, let me talk to their loved ones and piled facts one on top of another. I am eternally grateful to the lovely Spirit who brought me a buzzy bee, placed it in my hand and said 'give what you get'. He knew what I didn't. Buzzy Bee was his daughter's nickname at school. After she had left I thanked him for his kindness in delivering the final piece of evidence that made me certain he was there, along with my family members, friends and Guides.

I have watched many, many mediums doing the same as me. Wanting to put forward an alternative world view because we believe it based on the evidence of our own experiences, and because we feel it can transform a person's experience of life in a positive way. Developing good connections, learning how to express what can often come through as just a physical feeling or building up the energy required to communicate in a very different way take time, effort and patience. So I find it extremely disrespectful to be judged by people who have no idea what they are talking about. Let's be blunt. I've been told I cold read. I've been told my experiences are a load of rubbish. I've been told I'm guessing. I've been told I'm a fake, a fraud, a money grabbing vulture. And much, much more, most of it in a lot stronger language! But I'm not the only one who has been told this. Most mediums and psychics have been told they are simply tricksters preying on the vulnerable and gullible. My answer to all of these statements is 'walk a mile in my shoes'. I understand it is easier to fear, disrespect and dismiss what you don't understand. However, that seems to me to be the cowardly way out of expanding your understanding of things you don't currently want to face.

When I get armchair critics I send them loving forgiveness - they are judging something they aren't prepared to try to understand. Even if they are sitting within the spiritual community wanting to find answers, their defensiveness will prevent them from trying to communicate for themselves. We can all connect and communicate with one another intuitively through our natural ability to translate each other's psychic energy. It's a short step to talking to your own guides and loved ones. I get great comfort from this invisible network of support so why would I want to keep this to myself? Armchair critics will never be able to take that away from me - no matter how rude or judgemental. So, armchair critics, next time you expect a medium to 'entertain' you like a fairground sideshow, to tell you only what you want to hear or to be 100% accurate, consider the effort that person has put into developing this method of communication. My inner doubts have gone, so too, have my worries about external judgements. Let's move the discussion on to something more worthwhile.

Why do I do it?

How lovely to be able to help someone work something out; to draw from them the answers they always held; or, to create a flow of positive energy from myself to others. I suppose that's a part of the list of why I do public mediumship. There are also other things. My work will always involve a connection with Energy Beings. I can start a conversation, be able to offer some compassionate support in times of trouble.

It is a long journey through grief when we lose someone we love, especially if they have died. There are so many emotions, so much to understand and a hollow place in our heart that will never be filled. As a medium I can offer evidence that life continues after physical death. I can also offer messages from those in the Spirit World. Or it may be that I am in the right place at the right time to be able to say words that will acknowledge, validate or encourage someone in their grieving process.

Having lost both parents, I also understand how grief can bring a sense of guilt. Which person am I grieving for more? Has the passing of time blurred the edges of grief in one passing whilst the other is still too raw? Is it ok to stay stuck in my grief when others have apparently moved on? I have the blessing of knowing from the Spirits themselves what happens in the Afterlife. I can contact my loved ones at any time which is much the same as when they were here. If I can share this knowledge with others and teach them to pay attention to their intuitive senses then they too will find a way out of the stuckness of grief.

Another interesting aspect about my work is who steps forward to give messages from the Spirit World. People often expect their nearest and dearest. Sometimes they are surprised that a friend has come to speak to them. They wonder why that person and not a family member. People sometimes want only certain people to bring them messages, or have an expectation that only their close family will want to talk to them. So when they get a message from a more distant person they have connected to in their life they want to know why. They also worry about why someone they were sure would come through hasn't. I know it's disappointing. I know it can be upsetting. And I know that it doesn't seem right that the people we have been closest to couldn't or wouldn't step close. I've felt all those feelings waiting for my family members to connect with messages for me. After all, if they love you why wouldn't they make the effort. I can ask for significant people or specific people to come and connect. It's wonderful that eight times out of ten the Spirit people can respond to that request and the person most wanted by the sitter communicates. But there are still times when, despite my best efforts, the person who steps forward is not who the sitter wants.

I questioned my Guides a lot about this. Especially when I was waiting to hear from the people who I'd lost. Or when I heard from Gladys, the lady who was my training officer in my very first job so many years ago. I've sat in readings trying to find a yes to encourage the medium, hoping that I would recognise the Spirit person and wishing it could be my Mum or Dad instead. What the Guides told me time and time again was that the people really close to me had to make adjustments to being in the Afterlife. That they had to detach from wanting to speak to me like they had when they were alive. To the day my Dad died I was his little girl. The last time I saw him he was still trying to suggest ways in which I should run my life. Right now, to my Dad I am still his little girl. That means he very rarely comes to give me a message. He (and now I) understands that I have to make the best of my life according to my own free will choices. He can't influence my decisions - even if I'm going to fall flat on my face.

Until the Spirit loved one can speak in the message without actually saying what you should do they are still too attached to the Earth journey. They are helped and supported by family and Guides to find a more detached view. No less loving, no less concerned for us yet recognising our independence of choice. Often, they send a proxy (my Grandfather comes on behalf of my Dad). The Spirit who steps forward will always help to bridge the gap between both people so that comfort, confirmation and acknowledgement can be given on each side. That's why sometimes it's friends not family. Friendship can carry us through the challenges of life, sometimes more successfully than anything else, because it is a wonderful form of love. Friendship is giving and sharing too. Our friends are the people who are prepared to tell it like it really is. Our friends on the Spirit side still want to be here for us. They want to remind us of what we shared together. Most especially they want to show that time, space and eternity can't get in the way of a loving friendship. It is also true that Spirit people find other ways to connect with you. There are certain songs that connect me to my loved ones. It's amazing how often I hear those songs, seemingly randomly, just at the moment I need a loving boost. Or someone down here uses a phrase or two from someone 'up there'. Or an advertising hoarding, a bus number plate, a google search pulls a memory of a loved one in front of me.

Afterlife is Life

At this point I'd like to say what I know about the Afterlife, Spirit World, Heaven or any number of other names for where we head off to when we die. What strikes me about the many visions, near death experiences and channelled descriptions of life after death is that they are invariably positive. I did ask my Guides why there are no reports of hell. Was there a big secret being kept from all of us? Do those destined for hell struggle to come back? Or were those tales in sacred texts and visions something else entirely? I know it's a subject that worries many people, especially if they have certain religious views, and sets up a fear of dying. And it worries the loved ones of the people who pass over. If we hope for an Afterlife, we want it to be something that our loved ones will enjoy.

I talked earlier in my book of my personal experience of the Afterlife. Knowing that I had experienced a deep bliss and unconditional love in that vision, I was concerned about the idea of a place of punishment. Was what I saw a true place? My Guides were very keen to help me understand that the Spirit World is a place of unconditional love. It's a place where we choose to live a different life with the desire to be of service to one another. As well as to help and be of service to everyone we have left in the Earth realm. There is a process that every Spirit returning goes through. It involves healing from the wear and tear of being human. There is a life review where we get to see all that we have done from a perspective of the bigger picture.

Down here, we tend to judge ourselves on the details of our life that are immediately in front of us. In the Spirit World, we can see how much positive impact we have had on the lives of others. Every little bit of it. We can decide what we would like to do to help make amends for anything that we feel hasn't been positive. A Spirit progresses through a spirit life by being of service in the best possible way to balance karmic energy. In fact, for some loved ones there is quite a surprise. So often it turns out what we judged down here as bad, negative or wrong has turned out to be exactly the right thing in the circumstances of what has followed from those events. The Afterlife is aboutreviewing and rebalancing. Not eternal punishment.

When I give messages, I feel the joy that the Spirits feel in being of service both to the people in the Afterlife and their loved ones left behind. They step forward because they want their loved ones to know of a life free of human pain, judgement and sorrow. There is no fear or hate. Anger has gone. Instead there is peace, collaboration and creativity, where they can choose to do, be and have whatever they wish. Something difficult for us to find down here. I know from my Guides that it doesn't absolve us here on Earth from all the acts of unkindness we do. We still have to think about our responsibility for the actions we are taking. But they want us to think about the Afterlife as a chance to re-do some of our choices so that the energy we create is more positive. Even better if we were to start from right now taking full responsibility for what we do and try to be a source of positive thought, feeling and action.

Boundaries

I'm aware that I can get so caught up in the meaning and positive impact of messages that I can forget to have any life of my own Passing on accurate messages is a big responsibility. It matters so much to the people who need guidance, to hear from their loved ones or to have some hope in their lives, that taking my mediumship seriously is a key part of what I do. I try my very best to pass on the whole of the communication as clearly as possible. The Spirit people bring in their laughter and fun too so that is a lighter part of the connection. But like most people, when I'm working I know that underneath there is a responsibility to get the job done. So, every now and again my Guides will step in to drag my attention to the matter of boundaries.

I really admire Judge Judy Sheindlin. She is a lady with much wisdom, a ready wit and great intelligence. She has also lived a long life of service to others and learned a lot on the way. One of her quotes, in the TV court where she adjudicates civil cases, is 'My playpen, my rules'. She is amazing at holding her boundaries and earning respect from even the most grudging of participants. She is also extremely firm and not afraid to enforce her rules. I'm writing about her because the best quality she has, after her honesty, is her determination not to be too nice. She has a very clear focus about her role, her power and the need to balance her decisions fairly. So often the people who bring their cases find that they are being tested by sharp, pertinent questions. All so that the issues can be spelled out and the boundaries set. Judge Judy often pops into my mind when my Guides want me to watch my boundaries. I've already mentioned the Contract - the rules of our relationship. We can only work together as a team if we have give and take, respect and acknowledgement of our roles. There is another contract involved in working for Spirit though. That is the one between the person or people getting the messages and me.

This agreement can cover all sorts of things to help make sure everyone involved is working effectively for the best of all concerned. It's about being fair to each other. I work with my

Guides in the clear understanding that it is my playpen (my choices of when and where I work) though I will consider everything they ask me to do. And seek more information if I'm not sure what I'm being asked to do. It also follows that when someone approaches me for a message I ask them to work to my rules so that I can feel like I have given the best service I can in the best way I can. My main rule is about the way I work. I am an evidence based medium so I ask my Guides to bring me lots of confirmations. That tends to mean a lot of information is packed into each reading. I know from my own experience that it's hard to remember a whole reading anyway. Someone writing the information down as they get it is distracted from listening so a lot of information can still get lost. I always record my private readings. I hope that by doing so people will listen to the messages again and find comfort or new information as they do so. When someone says they don't want to be recorded, even if they are sitting in front of me, I will decline to do the reading. That is my choice as a professional.

Sometimes we are so keen to help that we will work under any conditions demanded by the person who has come to see us. I know that as, in my early days, I did just that. I answered the phone at 10pm, responded to the text at midnight or messaged back on Facebook at 6am. I replied to all of the unsolicited messages from people who hoped I would drop everything and give them a free reading. I was being nice. I was happy to help. Until I noticed that the requests didn't stop after the first time. Sometimes I was 'on call' for someone constantly. If I said I wasn't available in the instant they needed me, somehow I was in the wrong. That is when my Guides gave me a serious talking to. They asked me to consider my boundaries. To think about how helpful it was to wear myself out to the point where I wouldn't be able to help anyone.

They insisted I work out some rules for my work that I could live with. I now explain to people that I don't do unsolicited, free readings. If they want advice, information or support I am a professional person so will expect payment for my time. I also keep 'office' hours, so to speak, to make sure I get breaks when I can step out of the higher energies to relax. I only read for people when the energy is calm. If they are angry, defensive or closed to receiving a message it's my right to stop the reading. Or not begin it in the first place. I also have limits on how soon someone can have another reading. In my experience, the content of a message can take at least four or five weeks to be digested by the recipient. Coming back too soon means the person spends more money to hear what they have already been told to reflect on. And I certainly can't control the content of any message. I expect people to tell me as soon as possible into the session if they feel that the connection is not bringing them what they want. It might be because I'm not the right medium to make the connections for them. That does happen. I will happily suggest other mediums who they may want to go to. Finally, if the connection isn't working I will know within about five or ten minutes. It's my right to stop the reading. In those circumstances there is no charge.

So, Judge Judy appears every time I need to hold my boundaries. And that is still surprisingly more than you might expect. The conditioning to be 'nice' runs very deep. I am a deeply caring person but I have learned to balance caring for others with caring for myself. I say no a lot more often nowadays. And I follow my rules better. Stopping and thinking every time I get a reminder from my Guides. I hope that I will always have empathy for the person who feels they need something from me right then and there. Also, I hope that I will consider my rules before I leap into doing something just to be nice.

I have also expanded the ways in which I am 'in public'. My blog challenge has turned into a daily blog that is half way through its second year. I also do videos of channelled guidance once a week. I use social media to pass on the wisdom and answers I receive from my Guides. All of these are my ways of working for Spirit. They are not the only ways but my uncertain first steps into public mediumship have been rewarded. I know that many more people are receiving the help of the Energy Beings than might have been if I'd stayed in the background. It was a leap of faith. A big one. I am delighted that I took it!

SERVING A HIGHER PURPOSE

"There is a calling within each of us. A desire to make the world good. To see our family and friends happy and peaceful. We strive to change our life around to make it so. No matter what. Against all odds. The Spirit within us wants to shine the beauty of unconditional love, forgiveness, gratitude and service to all who are ready to share it. Being human is a powerful journey full of limitations or restrictions. It is our nature to rise above it all and shine our Light." Wolf Running

Learning wisdom – the teacher

Helping hand-Ups

Open to receive

Gratitude

Low vibrational days

Shadows

Psychic Art

The Down 2 Earth Heart Centre

Endings and beginnings

Learning Wisdom – The Teacher

As things moved on for me it seemed I was destined to be a teacher. One way or another my Guides tried to wangle it that I wound up teaching intuition and mediumship. I plodded on in my public mediumship describing myself as a spiritual counsellor, a pastoral counsellor, a facilitator and a spiritual coach; I was avoiding job titles like teacher, guru, master, lightworker, and oracle. It seemed to me that these titles often resulted in more stereotypical misunderstandings or the distinct secondary question of 'who says you are'. Then it was time for me to improve my ability to channel healing energy and clean up my own energy. As I explained earlier, off I went to become a Reiki Master/Teacher. More headaches about a job title. I had the certification to say the I was both a master and a teacher. But I was resisting that word 'teacher' still.

I've been very fortunate in my work for Spirit that I have had opportunities to learn a lot about myself. When I became aware of my intuition, of the way my energy was going out into the world and being in connection with all the other energies, I had a steep learning curve. I guess I've always believed that what you give you get back. Finally recognising my own energy giving and the way it was affecting what I got back was a real challenge. It was in the midst of all my own development that my Guides also asked me to start teaching about intuition and mediumship. When I look back from this point, I can see that they wanted me to learn by experience what being your authentic self actually means in practice. How could I offer, share and manage the energy of a group without realising what my own energy was up to?

We learn in several ways. I prefer reflection and experience. Or, much more my style of learning, reflecting on what I have just experienced. Not always the easiest, because in doing so you can have lots of failures or mistakes thus repeating the experience over and over. Thought experiments (often used in theoretical physics) are a way of reflecting on options so you can grow by exploring your inner self. You can model ethical options, consider what feelings certain experiences might arouse or identify outcomes that work for you. We can also learn by imitation. By copying what those around us are doing we learn how to talk in social groups, how to play football or paint. Of course, following what someone else has done appears easier. Much of the development work has been done for us, the prototypes have been tested and the glitches mostly ironed out. There are plenty of products that have taken an original idea and refined it to the profit of the person copying the inspiration.

When my Guides asked me to teach mediumship I was reluctant. What did I know about connecting with Spirits except what I had learned from my own experience? They insisted I consider becoming a teacher. They explained that I had gathered most of my learning by experience and reflection. They knew that I would rather not copy other people because I'm keen to know 'how'. Imitating someone else is the 'how' of what they do, not the 'how' of what I do. Learning the wisdom of connecting my way certainly has been the right path. I am proud to be an evidence based medium striving for accuracy in what I give to people in their messages.

I understand the 'how' of how I achieve that goal. I also understand what doesn't work. That's a really important point. It's the one that changed my life in a big way. There are choices we make when we are learning to be our true selves that lead us to a clearer understanding of our talents, skills and abilities. There are also choices that end up with us being lost in a forest of confusion about who we are and what our unique abilities are meant for. Pitfalls await. Yet the benefit of knowing what support you can offer through knowing yourself is wonderful. It's also been my pleasure to offer teaching support to a large number of people over the last nine years so that they can learn about themselves.

Here's some of what I've discovered about me, you, Energy Beings and connections.

Helping Hand-Ups

We often extend a helping hand. We want to support someone when we feel they are stuck, confused or heading towards a dead end. We feel that there is a way we can say or do something to help them make progress. Extending a helping hand, though, can be an interesting spiritual challenge. First, there is the decision how to offer help. What words do I use to show I care and am available to give support? Often, we may feel that we can see through the fog someone finds themselves in better than they can. We want to bring clarity to their situation. Yet is that really the case? It can be very easy to identify what I think the problem is, to offer what I think the solution is and to get it completely wrong. Does that mean I say nothing? I have certainly had to choose to say nothing. When there were outcomes of offering help that risked the relationship between me and the other person, I chose to support the relationship rather than the current issue. Even if it meant the other person had to struggle harder with something. Or when the support is accepted again and again but the other person doesn't seem to get out of being stuck.

As a Reiki practitioner, I was fascinated by the choice made by Dr Usui, the founder of modern day Reiki, to stop healing, for free, the beggars and poor people of Kyoto because he noticed that they didn't manage to change their lives in positive ways. In fact, it appeared that some preferred to return to ill health as they visited him again and again. Sometimes help can become a form of hand out. The person struggling with their problems accepts the temporary relief from those issues but returns to a place of stuckness. If we follow with Dr Usui, he suggests that people like this have not recognised the spiritual aspect to their problems. If I continue to extend a helping hand in those circumstances, I am becoming an enabler. I am enabling that person to stay stuck by providing temporary relief from the challenges they choose for themselves.

Are there limits to the number of times we should extend a helping hand? I would say that there have to be. To make spiritual progress we have to make an inner journey. We have to address why we limit ourselves, our relationships, our happiness and joy. I willingly give my time and energy to help people yet I often come up against a sticking point where what I say or do isn't what the person wants, expects or needs. It seems we are also very clear about the kind of help we expect to get, and what is given is ignored or dismissed. Helping is only progress if it's a hand up. When someone accepts what you can give rather than expects what you can't. When they can use what you offer to assist in that inner journey as well as in outwardly practical ways. I love to give hand ups; then I know that my time and energy are more likely to do good than harm. I look for the signs that someone is trying their actual best to help themselves. If I don't see that, I regretfully stop helping. There is no point to spending energy on someone who wants to stay stuck. After all, there are lots of people I can help who want to do the inner work.

Open to Receive

The other side of helping is receiving. It's one of the reasons I had to learn the difference between hand outs and hand ups. I believe many of us struggle to ask for help. I know I did and sometimes still do. I can feel my Guides raising their eyebrows as I admit this! It's part of the conditioning we have experienced but it is a real limitation to a positive flow of energy through our lives. We believe we have to solve every issue by ourselves because we have mostly become a society of individuals. What extending a helping hand can do is allow each of us to offer and accept support of some kind. Accepting is the biggest barrier we have to overcome. If I accept help I am choosing to let someone experience the joy of giving, or even learning how to give. All I have to do is be prepared to ask for and accept whatever is given.

I've learned that I need to step away from the way something is offered. I ignore the words that are used. That's because a refusal is much easier when I'm in the 'you just don't understand' mode. It's much easier to refuse when you have an excuse to hand. After all, we all struggle on alone at times thinking that it's the only way to get through difficult times. I'm much better now at accepting that the person offering won't get the whole of the issues facing me but they do want to make a difference for me. That difference could be a cup of tea, a listening ear, a gift of food or money or help in filling out forms. Whatever it is, I now know that I am making spiritual progress. I am choosing to be part of a community and showing that a hand up is always appreciated.

Gratitude

As I moved through the moments of learning and teaching about energy, one of the things I noticed was the way in which gratitude flowed out and back between people. One of the virtues of being here in human form is to be able to see how blessed we are. From my contact with the world of Spirit Beings and the Angelic Realm I believe goodness and the recognition of acts of goodness is one aspect of Divine bliss. Being grateful, is, I feel, a way to recognise goodness in our lives. Recognising the good, being thankful for the good and acknowledging it
to yourself and others is to share a small slice of the Divine bliss. In the past, I have found it hard to recognise the goodness and be grateful. I feel that is the case with many of us.

We are conditioned to feel lack, to compete and to live in a fear controlled way. We look for the reasons why we don't have happiness instead of understanding that happiness is a way of experiencing the world. We can choose happiness any time we want to step out of the fear. When I began to talk to my Spirit visitors they encouraged me to consider my life in more detail. They wanted me to slow down, pause and be aware of each moment as if it was my last. They asked me to think about my last moment as a human in this lifetime. Would that moment be a happy one? I found that a very hard thing to do. I was so locked into the past mistakes and the future fears that being right here, right now seemed impossible.

With encouragement I began to leave the past behind me. I realised that there was nothing I could do over. It was what it was. In looking to leave it behind, though, I had the opportunity to recognise how my past had shaped my present. I began to feel grateful for all the mistakes I had made, the things left undone and the opportunities missed. No matter what the twists and turns, somehow, I was still here, having time to be grateful for myself and all of the people who had already been a part of my life. Together we had chosen situations and experiences that had helped me know what misery and happiness meant to me. These good people had also presented me with the choices I now have in my life. Without their willingness to be exactly who they were I wouldn't know how I can do things differently. Or even perhaps that I have choices. As I started to work on gratitude about the goodness of my past - even those acts that I put myself through pain for - I became much more conscious of the present moment. That I have choices moment to moment about the way I am feeling. I saw a glimmer of happiness emerging from being in the moment. What was holding me back was my fear of the future.

One of the things I'm frequently asked about is to predict the future for people. Especially their financial and relationship future. These two issues are the ones that always seem to come up whenever people are talking. Stress about money and uncertainty about relationships cause an awful lot of soul searching for most of us. Yet our lives are a brilliant example of running away from the fact that they have to end. We focus instead on the practicalities. Earning a living, paying the bills, escaping on holiday, putting the children through school, college or university. These 'responsibilities' drive us forward. We are distracted from recognising the goodness in the moment we are in. Often we reach a stage in life where death is really knocking on the door but we are still wondering, did we miss the happiness somewhere along the line? My Guides talked a lot about a life well lived.
They wanted me to notice that each moment we have builds up into a long and happy life if we can notice the goodness. If we can be grateful for every extra moment we get.

Taking my lead from these discussions, I make an effort to notice gratitude given and received. I am learning the attitude of gratitude. As I see each act of giving and receiving, I am also inspired by the positive feeling it creates. For that moment, someone feels the goodness or returns the goodness. It may be a thank you, a bunch of perky daffodils, a warm hug, a compliment or donation in a jar. It doesn't matter what shape or form the gratitude takes. Someone, or me, is saying I appreciate your goodness. You have been kind to me. The connection between us is beyond the simple bond of being humans together. We are sharing an energy inspired by Divine love.

There is even gratitude in the rude words, angry conversations, judgemental statements and belittling comments. Each one of these reminds me that I have a choice. I can take myself into the low vibrational energy of shame and blame, accepting what is said as a reflection on me. Or I can take these as prompts to rise above the lack of love, of fear and of control. Happiness is what we create when our lives are lived in loving gratitude, when we practice small acts of goodness towards one another so as to create a wave of positive, overwhelming kindness. When we are kind to ourselves and others we can change our corner of the world. After all, isn't the spiritual journey all about arriving at a place of peace and contentment. Of radiating that energy inwards and outwards? That's my view.

Low Vibrational Days

I also have to recognise that some days stand out for all the wrong reasons. I believe that our energy flows around us and in to each other. That's why if one person is really negative a whole group of people can end up focused on negativity. The negativity gets passed on to everyone they meet, and on and on. If I find myself in a lower mood, perhaps stressed or fed up or angry, I consciously look for a way to be kind to someone. Can I let another car out in front of me at a junction? How about letting someone else go in front of me at the checkout? Or smiling at the lady who is serving me in the shop? Or, perhaps my favourite one, making some time to be a listening ear to someone. I'm challenging myself to practice random acts of kindness. Any of these things are my way of recognising I'm not giving out good energy so I'm going to find ways to change my mood.

I know that I aim to find as much positive in every day as I can. This is so the energy I share with everyone else is positive too. Sharing the positive has the result of bringing the amount of positive around me up a notch or two. It may even brighten up more than those around me. Random acts of kindness can balance out the flow of low vibration energy being sent out for all of us to share in. I can also give myself random acts of kindness. I can go and sit in the sunshine instead of finishing a task. Or I can spend some time reading my favourite quotes to energise myself. Or I can let the low vibration feelings have a bit of room, let them express themselves and love the part of me that is feeling that way. In the end, it's all about my choices. I can indulge the low vibrations and accept that I'm sharing them with everyone or I can work to change the way I feel and hopefully spread a nice wave of kindness around for all of us.

Shadows

Then there are the shadow times. We all have to work with situations inside or outside of ourselves that we think are black and white but often turn out to be anything other than clear cut. There is a shadow area where we can get lost in a loop of misunderstanding, half-truths and little or no reliable information. Bringing a beam of light into the shadow areas, lighting up the issues and making a more informed decision pushes the shadow choices away.

What do I mean? I can have a situation that I would like to respond to from a spiritual perspective. I want to offer all of the participants unconditional love, myself included. I would like my thoughts, words and actions to bring the light of truth to the issues. I don't want to cause hurt or harm but if I take no action then I will be the one potentially hurt or harmed. So how do I turn this around? How do I move out of the grey areas by taking the spiritual path? It always helps me to remove situations from the personal to the objective as much as possible. That way the drama that is being enacted won't necessarily suck me in. Of course, I'm human so my feelings and thoughts are going to be an important part of how I am going to respond. However, when I get stuck in cloudy energy I always ask my Guides to help me. Their help can light up the situation for me. It can push back the shadows and lighten me too.

Their message is always clear for me. When I'm sunk into fear, anger, worry or sadness and despair, they remind me of my true self. The bit inside that is pure Spirit. The bit that contains the Light I'm here to shine. Wolf Running will say:

"If someone or something is casting a shadow over you hold back from giving them or the situation any of your Light. You will dim yourself. Keep shining as brightly as possible. In the end your light will always chase the shadows away."

He, most of all, brings me the understanding that I'm a Spirit in a clay overcoat. The overcoat isn't what really matters, it's my Spirit self that I choose to express in the world of shadows.

There is another aspect to the shadow though. Having knocked about the world for quite a number of years now, I'm fascinated by the resurgence of 'spirituality' (my first experience of people describing themselves as spiritual was in the early 1970s). Faith religions seem to be struggling to hold onto or engage their followers. People in secular societies are seeking faith through an exploration of 'spirituality'. But what is it that they are getting? The Hans Christian Anderson fairy tale about the Emperor's new clothes is a lesson in illusion. The top person, leader, chief so wanted to show his status, wealth and power that he wanted what no-one else could afford. A pair of clever salesmen said the Emperor could have the finest, richest new clothes - with one special feature - they would be invisible to those who were either stupid, incompetent or not worthy of their position. Only certain people would be able to see or appreciate these magnificent clothes. It took the truth of a small boy to point out the Emperor was actually naked. All his ego and money had purchased was the false flattery of those who wanted to gain status and power for themselves without appearing stupid.

So too with spirituality. Many people announce that they have the 'true' path, the only way for you to live a perfect, happy, successful life. Just spend X Y Z or attend A B C and you will be initiated into the mystery of the path to success. So, with ego in hand, often saying inside 'I'm not worthy', we jump into a long journey with egos that are saying 'I'm better than you - I have the secret to a happy life'. But it's all an illusion - everyone is naked! A spiritual life is not about asking the God/ Goddess/Universe or anyone else to provide 'it' so we can feel happy, successful and well off. Nor is it searching here, there and everywhere for the truth that is right in front of your nose. It's about DOING so we can learn to BE ourselves and BE of service. Letting actions speak louder than the words we say. Living our values not just talking about them. What I realised from the people who speak spirituality but live in ego was that my journey also had to make its way through the shadow side of me and of life. Even with the best of intentions, with all sorts of positive energy as part of my giving and receiving, I'm being foolish if I ignore the other side of myself. We all need to make a trip to the dark side. If only to understand the consequences of our choices on ourselves and others. I finally became a much better teacher once I stopped avoiding the low vibrational thoughts and feelings that are part of me being human, and started working to acknowledge and release them.

Stepping away from my ego mind has been hard. After all, it has a job to do. It evolved to keep me safe. To ensure I survived so humanity carried on. It's an evolutionary imperative. However, my ego mind isn't bothered if I'm happy or not. Happiness isn't a necessary survival trait for my ego mind. It pushes me to do things through fear of not existing. It really isn't bothered if those things make me feel miserable. In modern times, there is so much fear but most of what we fear isn't life threatening. Yet we are driven. My Spirit is working hard to remind me that we exist for eternity in many different forms. And so do all of those people we love whilst we are down here.

My energy is eternal. It has and always will be. Finding a way to express my spirit energy has been consciously at the centre of my life for the last 11 years. I have learned to follow where my nose leads me, so to speak, knowing that whatever I encounter on this roller coaster ride of life is an opportunity to serve myself and everyone else. Public mediumship, teaching, healing are all the ways I have learned to express my unique contribution of energy. Never slow to move me ever onwards, just as I was settling into a comfortable rut, once again my Guides pushed me to a cliff edge.

Psychic Art

By 2009 I was here, there and everywhere demonstrating my mediumship, Intuitive connections and working with Energy Beings. Messages flowed out of me every day. Teaching workshops filled my weekends and spare evenings. My development was boosted by the self-healing I was regularly doing. I felt like I was fully occupied with my spiritual journey and enjoying every moment. Of course, it was the perfect time to throw in another cliff for me to jump off. That 'cliff' was my introduction to psychic art. This certainly produced a big wall of resistance as I firmly believed I was no good at any art form.

Naturally, my Guides began a program of softening me up. As usual. Rather tongue in cheek I went along with it because I was sure I would never produce anything resembling a painting, or other artwork for that matter. I knew I couldn't do art. I knew for sure. When I was thirteen my art teacher had told me not to opt for art as an 'O' Level choice because I wouldn't pass. If my teacher had said it then it must be right. From that time, I'd put away all of my paints, pencils, craft work and experimental daubings. No way would my Guides overcome this. Not even if they brought the best artists in to channel through me. I couldn't draw to save my life.

So, it began. Me sure I couldn't paint. My Guides insistent that I could. Every time I picked up a pencil I felt panic. If I had to get the paints out I was stressed. Every page I put something on got ripped up as I thought it was rubbish. Fortunately this didn't continue for too long. They sent me on a workshop. All about Angels. Nothing to do with painting. I assumed they had dropped the subject. No such thing. Working with another lady I found out that I had been paired with a portrait artist. A lady who could draw extremely well. Who also got a message from one of my Guides that I needed to paint. Pat is an incredible lady. She somehow persuaded me to go and visit her. Then she let me play with her paints. My lovely ArchAngel Seraphina painting emerged.

Somehow, I had overcome my resistance and reluctance. Pat

gently encouraged me to tune into the energy of my Guides so that it seemed easier to let the movements of the paintbrush flow freely. Seraphina was quite clear about how she wanted to be painted. I let myself trust that whatever I was doing would be ok. When I stood back, feeling that the energy had faded, I saw an angel sheltering me. Somewhat abstract but quite clear in its positive energy. I knew I had to return to painting. There was a force of creativity inside me waiting to get out, if I let it. The way to embrace it was to get playful with my paints and pencils. I drove home that day desperate to find a shop where I could buy canvas and more paints. I wanted brushes, pastels, charcoal, oils, varnish. Anything and everything. Of course, there was a shop in my home town selling just those kinds of things so you know where I headed as soon as I parked the car.

That was the beginning of a great creative journey. I have ventured into encaustic wax, dabbled with oils, mooched through acrylics and sploshed with watercolours. Each new venture was a step off a little cliff. For quite a while I kept saying that my work was rubbish. Then I painted something I really loved. When I took it to be framed the framer asked me how I had managed to get the shimmer background. He loved it and wanted to try the technique himself. From a fellow artist that was a big compliment. I felt so proud of myself to have done something someone else admired. I decided that I'd better start getting accustomed to the idea of being an artist. Maybe even displaying some of my work a bit more publicly. I bless all those friends who came to my house and had an impromptu presentation of my art. They were very patient with me.

Then I sold a painting. It almost broke my heart! Although it was wonderful to get a return I felt like I was sending one of my children away. Then someone offered to display some of my art. Could I let more of my children leave me? I felt reluctant until I realised that creativity brings that challenge. My Guides reminded me that there were more paintings to come. To them each painting offered another opportunity to send positive energy out into the world. More painters wanted to work through me creating items that individual people would benefit from. I resigned myself to selling my work half believing that it had no value. I was still struggling to release that hurtful judgement from so long ago.

It had hurt because I love art. Colour, movement, energy. I studied great painters from about age eight. Cezanne, Van Gogh, Picasso. Abstract, world seen sideways, open to interpretation, moving, colourful. I loved creating my own works. Mainly abstract because I loved the sense of freedom. What I found a challenge was drawing still life. I practiced all sorts of other styles. But not still life. That teacher thought art was all about faithful representation. Things had to look like what they were in life. No wonder she struggled with my abstract work. Instead of opening her mind she strayed into a judgement of me based on her prejudices. With negative effects.

I worked to forgive her. She's long gone to the Spirit World. Eventually I became braver. I started to trust what I could produce. Loving that it opened up an energy connection that spoke to people in a different way than messages or teaching. I started to run workshops on psychic art. Coming across others who had lost that child-like faith in the creativity within them. As I watched people rediscover the fun of dabbling with paint and pencils I knew that reconnecting to the arty part of myself had been a powerful healing for me. As I knew it would be for them.

One of my biggest projects has been to paint the energy vibrations of a group of ArchAngels. The Earth's ArchAngels started influencing my work with encaustic wax pieces. Although I had no idea that they were the beings behind the channelled work. All I knew was that some high vibrational beings seemed to be with me when I was using the wax in an abstract way. Yet when I was trying to use the wax to make things look like something recognisable it would end up messy. My shapes would be blobs splattered across the paper. All the colours would run. Only the abstract pictures drew my eye. Or felt right. Eventually when I moved on to canvas and acrylic I kept being urged to go for big pictures. That felt scary. Small canvas pictures were my comfort zone. But as always, when I let myself step out of that limitation I ended up with twelve amazing energy pictures. One for each ArchAngel. With a thirteenth that was their version of a group photo.

Art has become a wonderful part of my spiritual work. As a reward, I have had some success with my paintings and pastels in the Calderdale Open Art competition over the last three years. My pieces have made it into the exhibition. One of them won a prize. I've also had my work on display in the Hebden Bridge Open Studios events for the past three years. It's interesting to see how people react to my psychic art. And discuss the pieces with them. Especially, to find out what they see in my abstract pieces. I've also got myself used to selling my babies. I know they are going out into the wider world charged with positive vibrations for whoever is drawn to them. It's been very pleasant to get confirmation that certain pictures have reminded their purchasers of loved ones.

The Spirit World really does get everywhere.

The Down 2 Earth Heart Centre

Four years ago I needed to find a new place to work. I had done most of my teaching and readings in my home. However, I had moved to a much smaller house so something else was needed. Prompted by a discussion with a business advisor I looked around the town I consider to be my home. My association with Hebden Bridge has lasted nearly 25 years so that's where I started my search. Of course, nothing happens by chance. I came across a suite of two rooms with perfect light so that I could teach, do private readings, healing, paint and have an office space. On the day I looked at the rooms there was another suite right next door that shared an interconnecting door. I looked at the other suite and immediately saw a use for each one of the three rooms. I wanted both sets of rooms. I could only afford one. What to do? Of course, I threw the question out to my Guides. Who stayed silent. I eventually chose the set of rooms that would be right for my painting and started moving in. One day when everything was finally set up I sat down in the big group room where I was going to teach. One of my lovely Guides sat down next to me with a big smile. Hold the thought, she told me. What thought I wondered. The one about next door, she replied. When you are ready it will be yours. When will that be, I asked. Silence. Quiet laughter. That's up to you, I heard. So, a challenge and a potential new direction on its way in.

I soon settled into my stride in the new place. I was delighted to discover the spur of a ley line right through my large room. It was interesting having to balance the energy flow when teaching or doing trance mediumship. Some days it was so powerful it took a whole crew of Guides to hold me steady. One or two people appeared who wanted to rent a room and they used the large room too. By the end of the year there were several people looking to rent a room. On the point of renewing my rental I decided to take another look at the rooms next door. As I walked in once again my mind was full of ideas. I could see a Centre. A place for people to drop in. Some healing on offer. A room to develop my physical mediumship. More opportunities to teach. A way to provide a listening ear for spiritual counselling. Or just explaining what intuition and mediumship is all about. A down to earth place to step out of the world for a while. No wonder I rushed back and sent in an offer for the rooms. Six weeks later my Centre was a reality!

I've always looked for ways to let people understand that our intuition is a natural part of us. Ways that are accessible and not dependent on having money for exotic treatments, complicated workshops or loads of text books. I was sure that being able to provide hospitality and a comfortable space to relax was the key to prompting people to ask the questions they carry in their heads. After all, I had loads of questions throughout my journey. Sometimes I struggled to find a place I could ask them or anyone who could answer in clear and simple ways. At the back of my mind, busy being built in my dreams, was a psychic school. I knew there would be one. I had dreamed it more than eight years before. However, I was also sure that my kind of school would be experiential, non religious and focused on supporting individuals to take that inner journey of self discovery. Setting up a Centre would give me the foundations of the school too.

As with everything undertaken from a spiritual perspective there was still a huge journey of my own personal growth too. I let the rooms to help pay the rent. Holistic therapies vied with psychic work for space to grow. There was a great debate amongst the practitioners who used the rooms. They felt that because I had the word psychic in the title of the Centre it was putting people off. I eventually changed the name. I learned from this debate that I didn't have enough trust and faith to stick with my dream. Practitioners came and went, disappointed that the Centre didn't provide them with a client base. I learned that people may say they understand your vision but putting it into practice is something else. I also learned, once again, that we human beings have competition coded into our DNA. Or at least our ego mind is set on fighting for scarce resources. Managing my own, and other people's expectations, brought me to a big review of my own ideas of what spirituality means. Is it even possible to run a spiritual business? There were times when both ideas seemed distinctly at odds with each other. Time after time I found myself going back to my basic beliefs, to what I had learned as a child and throwing the questions and doubts to my Guides for answers.

The answers were long on coming but the experiences piled one on another. I know that working in the Centre has been a healing journey too. I have removed many layers of my own masks. I have been supported to face my fear and do it anyway. I have been challenged to stick with it. To show that I really, really want my dream of a psychic school. Many of the events of the last three years have brought me a much clearer vision of what has to happen, how it will be and who might share that particular journey with me. Not everything I have tried has been successful; I've got it wrong plenty of times. So, at times, it's a bit hard to believe that my Centre has been open now for over three years. That's not long by comparison to my mediumship (into its twelfth year in public) or my counselling (into its nineteenth year). Yet the Centre represents all of the amazing things that can happen when you find a little bit of magic.

One of the most surprising things I have learned was the way in which the energy I was working with and bringing into the Centre had a way of stripping people of all their masks. It's very hard to be authentic in a world where we are used to hiding ourselves in plain sight. We cover up our true feelings, hide our anger or sorrow and fear being found out. All of this stems from a feeling of lack. People who have visited find an energy space where the mask slides off as do the inner feelings. They have walked in burdened down by life and gone back out refreshed, energised, ready to take part in life again.

I know my Centre works, yet I wasn't sure that we could get to our second anniversary. The year 2015 was hard in many ways, with a lot of clearing of energy going on for me, the practitioners and the world in general. Then the flooding on Boxing Day 2015 in Hebden Bridge nearly knocked all the stuffing out of me and left many of the local people in challenging conditions. Yet as I celebrated our second birthday in 2016 with a host of visitors there were tears, laughter, warmth and compassion shining amongst the many conversations. I watched as, magically, new connections were made amongst people who were meeting for the first time, long established friendships brought reminiscing chats and a wave of positive love filled the room.

I finally saw what I have worked for all this time. The Centre has its own tribe. A like-minded community of very different people. People who want to take time out of the busy world for a while and share with others. A community is made up of people and the best sort is one that cares for all its members unconditionally. I have always believed that connecting people to one another was the best way to bring out the natural desire we feel to be helpful. Making that connection in a warm, homely and friendly environment helps everyone to remove the masks they might otherwise wear. The support, interest and genuine care that my visitors shared with one another was a powerful confirmation for me that I'm doing something good.

Powered by that positive celebration of all that is best about my Centre I turned towards a third birthday. Once again changes came along. It became clear that my model of a spiritual business needed a few tweeks. Some people are further along in their journeys than others. Holistic treatments drew the energy from my focus on intuitive growth. In the third year I found that neither I or the practitioners and visitors were sure what the purpose of the Centre was. Rooms became an interesting debate. Which one had the best, right or most favourable energy? Who wanted to work where? Once again, I threw questions at my Guides. How to make sure that the Centre continued to offer a retreat for those who had a spiritual need? Or a spiritual question. I went backwards and forwards with options. Yet my intuition kept reminding me to be true to my original vision. A place of learning where people could find out about their own personal energy, growth and intuitive abilities. I took the step of releasing the other set of rooms and moved myself fully into the Centre. Now my focus and attention are wholly on the Centre I am sure there will be more growth of that vision.

I couldn't do that without support. Each step of the last three years there have been other people and Energy Beings who stood with me, encouraged me and helped me develop my vision. That's another magical thing. When you work with honesty, ethics and a shared belief in doing the best you can, the focus shifts from competition to collaboration. From me/me to us/us. I hope that this intuitive tribe keeps on growing. There is a shift of perspective happening right now. We are all being urged to explore our intuition so we need to start understanding what it is that we already have. It's time to work forward in a positive energy. To do that we need a place where we can leave the old, negative beliefs and values behind. We need support and connection with all sorts of people, Guides and Energy Beings. My Guides say it's very simple. We need to rediscover Love. The power of love. Love for ourselves and from that the love for and from others. My journey in building this Centre has been a labour of Love.

Endings and Beginnings

A lot of my work is about letting go. Helping people to send their loved ones on a new journey down a road that we can't travel with them. Encouraging someone to fly free in one way or another. I miss my Mum and Dad being here on the Earth with me. I'm sure they could offer me support about being a parent and having to push my child out of the nest. Each day of her life from babyhood she is moving a step closer to independence, to her own life choices, to making her life what she wishes for herself. She has to fly for herself. She has to be free. In the same way that my parents had to ensure I found my own freedom, I have had to let her go, bit by bit. There have been times when I wanted so much to pick up the phone to my Mum and ask what do I do now. Or see my Dad who always made me feel like I was still his little girl. However, we have to let our loved ones pass away. In fact, we have no choice. It just happens, often when we feel least prepared for it to do so. We wish we had time to say one more thing, ask one more question or do something to show our love once more. We want to hold them close to us for as long as possible. We sometimes cling to our last conversation, last sighting, last moments. As if we can hold back the realisation that our world has changed forever.

Life does change though. In our beginning is written our ending. The door to the Spirit World is one we must all pass through. I talk about the Spirit World, bring messages from that world and give evidence from the Spirits who speak to me so that people can understand that there is another life, a new journey and a return to our loved ones. On this side of life, we are setting our loved ones free not to an empty, cold place or to non-existence but to a vibrant and loving new life. And we will be joining them when it's our turn to walk through that door. I love the quote by Paulo Coehlo "If you love someone, you must be prepared to set them free". Sending our loved ones off with our blessing that they step joyfully into their new lives is a wonderful gift we can give them. We may be overwhelmed by our own grief at their passing but we can wish them a good journey.

Releasing them to the Spirit World can have surprising results. It is wonderful to talk to people who have been able to sense the presence of their loved ones, or get a sign or even a message. In my case I found that my Mum was working with me as a Guide. I still have the loving connection with her that means I know when each person I care about is safe home in the Spirit World. I get the 'gossip' about what they are doing now as if they are still here on Earth. Our loving connections continue. When I started writing this book one of the things I focused on was what I loved about my Mum and Dad, as well as the good memories of precious moments, the laughter and the encouragement they gave me. They passed away at the time when my connections with the Spirit World were becoming more noticeable and harder to ignore. Both of them would have been a bit anxious about my new beginning yet keen to support me as much as they were able. I'm not a perfect person - neither were they - but some of my good bits come directly from the freedom they gave me. They got me out of the nest, flying free and making my life for myself. They also encouraged me to understand the value of service to others. Of the desire to bring comfort and understanding. Even of the need to have a purpose in life and stick with it. I've surely tested all of those values in my time.

I've been used to thinking that I needed a plan, a route and a destination through my life. Going off into the unknown has felt scary or like I was breaking some invisible set of rules. Yet a destination that's new can be so rewarding. Life isn't always like a return trip, even if we have been around in a lot of lives before this one. It's often a range of routes to an imagined destination that might or might not be there when you get to it. The only certainty is that at some point your journey will have one final end. Once I started to adjust my thinking about where I was going, my journey got easier and easier. There is only one actual final destination for me. I will be going into the Afterlife ready to start a new journey. The bit between setting off and getting to my death is about doing the best I can to make a smooth journey for myself. No matter what diversion signs I've followed, the u turns, pit stops and straight stretches I want to keep moving forward. The destinations between birth and death have been interesting so far and I'm looking forward to lots more stops. Now I don't have to worry what those stops will be. I can appreciate there will be times for me to rest and refuel, times to appreciate the view and times to share with my travelling companions. That is the most wonderful thing. We are all on the road together. It has helped me to realise that there are no rules to this journey. Each connection we make with one another is part of the plan, where that connection takes us is the route we follow through life and the destination of life is all about love.

So, it's also true that built into our ending are many beginnings. My exploration of my intuition led to a new beginning with mediumship. My journey into mediumship brought me self-healing and self-acceptance. These two benefits gave my dreams a new beginning because I brought the foundations of my purpose into the material world. I rediscovered my creativity through painting and writing. These are now solid objects in my world.

I have experienced the new beginning of working with the Earth's ArchAngels and the Centre that is the base for my psychic school. Being able to work with people across many situations gives me an opportunity to let them see that I'm an ordinary, down to earth human being. I can talk about what I do in a straightforward way. I can laugh about all the jokes about psychics. Because they have been in contact with me people have some knowledge about what and who a medium or psychic is. If they do decide they want to find out more, they have a contact they can use. Or if they want to explore their own abilities there is a way, through me, to get suggestions or support. There is a way they can open doors they perhaps hadn't thought to explore. Who knows what other new beginnings are waiting for me just around the next bend. I know I'm better able to welcome those opportunities, to want to grow into someone new. The last 11 years have been a roller coaster ride that I wouldn't have missed for the world!

The Last Word?

I set off writing this book with all sorts of good intentions. Two years ago I stepped off the cliff of becoming a writer because my Guides arranged for someone to ask me to write an article. As Helen is a lovely lady I said yes. I've been in every edition of her Valley Life Magazine since. Then came the blogging challenge. My good friend Jan is responsible for getting me into that. But I knew what my Guides were up to. Getting me to take small steps so that I would reach the edge of the cliff. I've had at least one book about mediumship inside me ever since I sat down in 2007 to write my first workshop workbook. I just didn't know how, what, why, when. Or how to begin getting it all out of my head. Because there is a lot packed in there. So much knowledge, wisdom and experience that they have made sure I've accessed. However, I have suffered from massive writer's blocks. As well as personal ones.

I have always been the reluctant medium. It's time for me to own that and to be clear where that comes from. I know that in past lives I've been given the gift of sight, divination, prediction. Call it what you will. I also know that those abilities have got me into deep water. Even brought about my death. My wisdom has been misinterpreted, manipulated and disrespected. I know it took my Guides quite a bit of effort to get me down here again. I also know that at one point I would cheerfully have left. But I feel driven to have this experience. And there have been many rewards.

So why has it taken me so long to put my words out in the form of a book? I'm settled into a daily blog. It's part of my pattern. I've run four writing challenges of my own to encourage others to find their authentic voice. I sent this manuscript off for editing nearly ten months ago having had to put fingers to keyboard over a short, sharp week of writing it all down once and for all. Surely it should have been plain sailing? Yet there was that cliff looming. So the long wait between first edit and final manuscript is me getting used to someone else reading my words about me and my journey. Like most of my leaps I've had to battle myself. Backwards and forwards. And to reassure myself that it will be ok to speak my mind. To say what I believe and hold my opinion when others disagree.

I'm thankful for my Guides who got me to this point. To my daughter who is busy writing her sixth book. To all those who have helped me by being my inspirations to deal with my stuff. I'm grateful that I am ready to birth this book and launch it into the world. I have no idea where it will end up but I do know that the freedom to write has come from this achievement. Without my intuitive abilities, I feel my life would have been more confused and lacking a direction. I have no idea where I'm headed next but the journey will be an adventure I'm looking forward to.

Was I lost? No question,

Did I know where I was? Not at all.

Had I ever been happier in my life? Never.

by Mary Oliver

If you have enjoyed reading about Annie's journey there are lots of ways to keep in touch with what she is doing now. Her web site is www.annieconboy.net. You can search and read nearly 700 of her daily blogs, purchase her artwork and CDs or make an appointment with Embrace Intuitive Mentoring. You can contact Annie by email at admin@annieconboy.net, or by following or friending her on Facebook, Twitter and Instagram. Her Facebook page Letters From The Light Side has a regular weekly live video with guidance for the week ahead. Or you can also find her videos on her YouTube channel. Her one to one work is through Embrace Intuitive Mentoring and you can also follow that page on Facebook.

Annie's next book is called Down 2 Earth: Awakening Intuitive Ability which will be available in May 2018. If you would like to read a little bit more right now there are a few of her blogs on the following pages. We hope you enjoy them.

DIVE INTO THE BLOGS

In the Kingdom of the Blind

Feelings: Mine, Yours, Theirs

Conversation in the Square

Exploring the Energy of 2017

Choosing the Energy of the Next Nine Years

In the Kingdom of the Blind

On of the more challenging things about opening up my psychic ability has been that I now 'see' energy. Not quite in the way I would through clairvoyance (clear seeing) where my third eye sees in the same way as my physical eyes. Through my clairsentience (clear feeling) I sense energy and my brain translates that feeling into an image or information for me. The information I get in that way is the true state of things - it's not possible to hide behind a polite smile or poker face. It's taken me a long time to get used to being able to 'read' people in this way as I can actually spot the stuck energy people carry around with them. Then I have to think if the information is at all useful. Or if I'm supposed to do anything to help them

get unstuck. I often say to people **'In the kingdom of the blind the one eyed man is king'** (Desiderius Erasmus) - I can see but what to do if no one else can?

Today, as every day, I switch my intuitive senses to closed as I go about doing ordinary things - housework, driving, paperwork, shopping. It's unfair to view people's aura energy as it really is. We all carry thoughts, feelings, hurts, fears, worries and much more in our personal energy field (the aura). We also carry the thoughts, feelings, hurts, fears and worries of others in that same energy field. Every time we interact with each other the energy between us shifts and moves around. There is no point, as far as I can see, in being the one eyed man at these times. People really prefer not to see what is under their nose (or in their aura) as it might mean that they have to change or do something differently. How many times have I told myself that I will write a daily blog and ended up not doing so? It is only happening now because I've found a way to help myself change out of a stuck energy state of no writing to a fluid energy state of writing

What brings this reflection to mind today is yet another example of someone receiving information about their energy state and deciding not to accept it. There are times when I do have to suggest to someone that they have a buildup of negative energy that needs to be released. Working intuitively as a healer or counsellor or teacher the energy in the relationship dynamic is really important. If someone is struggling to understand why they continually self sabotage themselves (as we all do to a certain extent) helping them to understand what is in their aura energy can lead to positive ways of releasing the energy. Volunteering this information is not my style - I wait until the person seeks my help before I explain about their energy flow (or lack of it). However, unless the person wants to have a clear energy field there is nothing further I can do.

We are all good at hiding from ourselves. We have all forgotten that lovely Spirit spark that sits inside the human overcoat. We judge ourselves and often, to avoid ourselves, pass those judgements on to others. Yet there is so much we can achieve if we are prepared to lift our own blindfold even

for a few seconds. Taking a good, hard look at ourselves, even if only with one eye, allows us to remove all the cruddy energy we have accumulated. That energy slows us down, holds us back and, in the end, turns into physical dis-ease. Yet there are things we can do, each and every one of us, to create a truly positive energy field to live in.

Becoming one-eyed is much easier than people imagine. It starts from noticing what you are feeling and thinking. You can help yourself by tuning into what your gut tells you - your intuition is feeding you information every second of every day. You can notice when you feel the lie a person just told you. Or that moment when your though says 'That's a lie". You can

learn to trust the information. I will not challenge a lie, though I might make a note of it to myself, unless the outcome of what I've been told has consequences for me. You can also acknowledge all the thoughts and feelings you are holding onto that weigh you down. If you are angry work through it. If you are fearful overcome it. If you are depressed reach out for support. If you are lonely ask yourself why you have excluded others from your life. You also might find that these thoughts and feelings aren't even yours.

Energetically we all live in the same ocean whether that flow is high energy or low energy. If you are surrounded by people who have a low energy flow then that is the energy you end up sharing. Some people are content to stay in the low energy because they feel it's all they know. But you don't

have to. You can find the high energy flow if you clear your own aura and protect it from taking on more negative energy. I switch my 'eye' on because with it I can tune into Energy Beings who have higher positive energy flows. They are happy to share their energy with me, to help me clean up my aura and to encourage others to do so. It was hard to look in

the mirror and see how far I had drifted from a positive energy flow yet it has been a wonderful thing to become a 'one eyed man'. Not for power or glory. Simply to show others how we can all benefit from being able to see with one eye. Is it time to take your blindfold off?

Feelings: Mine, Yours, Theirs

One of the questions I'm often asked is about how I know what Energy Beings are communicating. For me it all started with noticing my feelings. And then realising that some of them didn't belong to me.

In fact it's one of the things that I explain very early on when I'm teaching. Perhaps because I had to develop as a medium from my claresentient ability. All that time I spent working out if it was my pain in my back, or the back pain the Spirit person was trying to tell me they had, did eventually pay off.

I became very aware of my own feelings when I was working. That helped me to be aware of my feelings when I wasn't working too. It made me aware that I often soaked up other people's emotions. So much so that I got muddled most of the time.

Realising how much my psychic senses were switched on all the time I began to understand that I needed to sort all the emotions out. Sometimes a person with a strong ability to tune in to other people's feeling is called an Empath. Highly empathetic people can have real difficulty switching off

the emotional energy from everyone around them. In the same way, I can also switch into how Energy Beings feel. As I learned more and opened more to the messages I was getting I knew I had to protect my own energy.

Since we have feelings all the time I knew I had to be able to close off from other people's feelings.

Sifting through what I was feeling every day made me much more aware of what was my stuff and what wasn't. So I started to ignore the feelings that seemed to belong to others. I also made an effort to be in a bubble of positive energy. If I knew I was positive any negative feelings that popped in were suspect. Of course there are always going to be times when I'm negative about things. But being aware of and thinking about my emotions really helps to own only mine. I also learned to work with the intention to mirror back any feelings that weren't mine.

Imagining myself surrounded by mirrors I could reflect back those stray, random emotions. It meant my inner world became a lot clearer and much more manageable. Strong emotions are still a part of me but those are all mine. And I'm happy to deal with what I feel. Especially as I work to release the emotions in a way that doesn't send them out into the world. I know that if I radiate energy outward it will come back to me. So I want to have the positives coming back. And not anything else.

This carries into my work with Energy Beings too. At the beginning I could easily be swamped by the emotions they were sending me. It was all information to help me describe them. But it could be too overwhelming at times. Especially if they were experiencing an emotion I was feeling too. So that I could connect for them I had to ask for an agreement that they came in very gently. That they let me acknowledge the emotional energy gradually and that it cleared as soon as I had given it as information. Over time it has become possible to pick up the emotional information from very small blasts of energy.

So now I only get extra feelings when I'm tuning in for work. The rest of the time I'm protected from confusion, over-reactions and mistaking mine for theirs. I still feel. And react. But now I own that it's all my own stuff.

Conversation in the Square

Many of my messages come through a conversation. Either the person I'm talking to says something that I know is from Spirit. Or they tell me I've said something they really needed to hear. Or recognise as being from a loved one in Spirit.

Standing chatting in the Square this afternoon I was enjoying the sunshine. Our conversation was about that thorny subject - what is mediumship? As I talked I felt a familiar tingle. My Guide, Wolf Running, had his hand on my head. And next to me was a Guide belonging to the other person. I knew what I was saying had significance for both of us. So I listened carefully to the words that were falling out of my mouth. It was interesting to hear a reminder of why I started developing in the first place. And why I continue to share my knowledge about intuitive abilities.

Back in the beginning I was mostly curious. I wanted to understand what was happening. Why did I feel tingles at certain times? How did I seem to know what was going to happen? Or that a client was surrounded by loved ones from Spirit. Yes, I was already helping people through my counselling. I moved in that direction when the corporate world became too toxic and uncaring. As I opened up to the information from my intuitive senses I became more involved. I wanted to understand at a deeper level. Because I felt I had found a better way to help people. That's how I fell into mediumship. Somewhat reluctantly but going with it all the same.

The urge to help is very powerful in all of us. I know I have a conversation with myself every time I am around people who are stuck, lost or floundering. I want to somehow make it better.

As I continued into the connection with Spirits I found I was better than average at it. Still reluctant to believe in myself (or them) I fell into demonstrating and giving messages one to one. That's when I hit a big challenge. My need to help was fed by my Ego Mind. It told me how much better I could help by making sure I was the one people heard. There was a sort of competitive edge that wanted to creep in. I had a hard conversation with myself once again. Using my abilities was about being of service. Not being the big I Am. I decided then that when I was asked I would serve to the best of my ability. That's how I found myself teaching. Reluctantly. But reminding myself it was because of choosing to serve others.

Lots of things I have done have been in the background. Quietly. A conversation with one person. A message to another. A healing thought to a third. Visiting places when asked to by Spirit. Connecting people when required. Encouraging people to move on when the time was right.

Because to me mediumship is a whole lot more than standing on a stage just to flatter my ego. The temptation was certainly there. But I'm glad I resisted. That's not to say that everyone who works publicly is doing it to feed their ego. I know many wonderful mediums who serve day in and day out in public settings. They are there because it's their form of service. It's what has been requested of them. But I want to add a note of caution. A few aren't serving anyone but themselves

That's a sad conversation to have. To recognise that their Guides have to wait until the Ego Mind has run it's course. And hope that not too much damage has been done to the public in the mean time.

I encourage people to recognise mediumship in all of it's forms. Including the healers, psychics, Tarot readers, geomancers, intuitives, and empaths (amongst many names) who might cross your path. Along with the ordinary, kind hearted and open people who offer you support and encouragement when you most need it. They are serving too. Quietly. For no visible reward. Passing on the love that is all around if we choose to be open to it. I believe that intuitive ability is natural for all of us. And I also believe that when required we are all of service on behalf of Spirit. It's just that we don't recognise it. Or know how much our help has mattered.

The Spirit World would like to thank you today for everything you have done on their behalf. And ask you to keep doing it.

Exploring the Energy of 2017

Well, it's turning into an up side down week! The cosmic chaos of the next energy wave has already started to hit so I've very much been going with the flow.

Feeling energised and exhausted all at the same time has become a bit of a way of life for me this past three months. The planet and all of us are slowly shifting gear. I know it's time to get on with my spiritual mission. Yet I can't seem to see through the fog yet. I'm still groping around in the dark looking for the light switch most of the time. Of course there are occasional flashes of light. When I am exploring the energy stream heading to us from 2017 there are bright flecks of illumination. The trick is to catch the inspirations and act on them. If I do so I will be setting myself a good year ahead.

So how do I go about exploring the energy coming in? First of all, I am very aware of energy signals. For the last ten years I have been out and about every week connecting to the energy flow on behalf of other people. Before that I mainly connected in for myself through Tarot, meditation and conversations with my Guides. Learning to tune in on a daily, even hourly basis, has helped me read the energy stream more and more accurately. Secondly, I am open to the reality that the energy flow has many currents. It is a hotch potch of criss crossing intentions, feelings and thoughts all muddled up together. That's why using the Law of Attraction often ends in disappointment. Shaping energy requires a clear, unequivocal intention. Not something I always find easy to do.

Then I have to consider that what I am exploring might be the energy flow belonging to other people. We are all connected. How much of what I am sensing relates to the people I care about the most?

Wishful thinking can distort what I pick up. Perhaps my daughter wants me to make certain choices that suit her? Maybe my aunty hopes that I will do something that fits with her agenda? In the muddle of energy I have to sort out what belongs to me. Then I can be ready to accept what it brings

in. And that's the fourth thing. I have to be open to recieve what is coming my way. That's not quite as easy as it sounds. I remember being told I should develop my mediumship. There were opportunities for me to do so. I sat on the fence for a very long time. Not ready to receive that experience. Or to take actions that I understood might change my life forever.

Even then I was being intuitive! I sensed that exploring my psychic ability might have a deep impact on my beliefs and way of life. Since I wasn't quite sure if that would be positive or not I sat back and refused to take action. Not quite the brave explorer I had always thought I was. But I learned. I learned to notice the prompting of my intuition. The flow of energy eventually immersed me in new information. Out of it came some amazing leaps forward. Now I'm back to another set of leaps. 2017 is an Ascension year. What I begin next year will change my life once more.

I know that, even if I don't know exactly what I will be beginning. I've moved from Growth Into Awareness to Growth Into Ascension.

It's scary, exciting and an adventure. I suspect it's going to be another wild ride. Ten years ago I approached the energy of change that had entered my life with a lot of nervousness. I was unsure what would turn up in the fog around me. This time I can't wait. The little glimpses I have had are amazing. I really do want my chance to go exploring and have an escapade or three. There are others joining me on the journey. What a fab way to connect to each other. So it's time to travel light, travel free and travel with joy.

Choosing the Energy of the Next Nine Years

This has definitely been a Nine year. Full of upset, endings, parting of the ways and closure. Also full of reflection, truth and searching. As a Nine person I can find a Nine year more of a challenge than most.

That's why today I needed a bit of help with making sense of it all. So much has happened to me on an inner, personal level this year. A lot has gone by in a blur. Often I've felt like I've bounced from one situation to the next, steering myself purely by what it felt right to do at the time. Thinking about ending this year and how I want my December to be I realise I want it to be very different than all those other Decembers of the last nine years.

And the ones before it back to when my Mother died. That changed December in a very big way for all of my family.

As I write this blog I recognise that an important anchor went with my Mother. Yet she came back to me as a Guide. I had to become independent in my human life whilst we shuffled the relationship around. Then we could work together without compromising my free will choices. She has been very much around in the past couple of weeks. Along with my Nanna, her mother, my Dad and other family members. They have been standing strong for me while I worked out what I learned about myself this year. And then began working out what I want 2017 to be for me.

As the energy of new beginning approaches I know that the Universe is offering me anything I want. I have so many options. But there is the trap. Do I revert to old habits, my comfort zone, which means I stay restricted. Or do I seize the new?

It's an important decision. I know that I will be setting up the energy for the next nine years by the choices I make. In fact that's true for all of us. Even if I get a huge blast of new energy, if I'm not careful, I am going to be containing it in my old patterns. Of course that won't work. The new energy will fade away due to my old choices.

New energy will carry me forward over the next nine years only if I invest it in new beginnings. Not the trick of seeing the old as new. But the clear sightedness of recognising something as genuinely being new. So back to thinking about what I've learned about my patterns in the last nine years.

Sometimes I need a prompt. This afternoon I got out my tarot cards. An old, familiar friend when I'm stuck. My thoughts were all over the place. I asked in my mind for help. What could the cards tell me, and everyone else, about this new year? Of course, I ended up pulling card number one in the Major Arcana. In my pack it is called Awareness (the Magician in other interpretations). As I read the information these two sections stood out: "This card is one of the key reminders that you already possess all of the tools to guide and direct you in your life." 'This card represents your ability to create your own reality - to set ideas into motion and watch them grow."

I was smiling to myself as I reached for the next card. It's true. I know so much more about myself, my abilities and skills than I did at the start of this nine year cycle. And I'm ready to use my wisdom to create my dreams.

The second card I got was also in the Major Arcana. It was Fertility (the Empress in other packs). Once again I looked to the information in the book. I read "Through this card, the manifestation of growth is on the horizon. You're the creator, and the seeds that have been planted in the past ... are now ready to give birth into your world. Be patient as you watch your seeds take root and grow. Nurture them as they become strong and healthy." I have certainly had a lot of new dreams this year. When I've been coping with the challenges of bringing my Spirit being more fully through into my human being I've imagined as much positive as I could. I've known I needed more than me to get my dreams into reality.

The people and Energy Beings around me have been a key part of my choices. Their support, actions and reactions have informed what I've done. And what I have chosen for my future. Feeling like I am grounded back in to a clear vision I know that I will be stepping as far out of my comfort zone as I can reach. I'm saying yes to the scary new. The safe new is a trap I want to avoid. Sometimes my inner intuition is scrambled. Like today. How wonderful to see my way by using the gift of the Tarot. In two days it's the birthday of Margaret. She was the Earth Guide who introduced me to reading cards 24 years ago.

I like to think that from her place in the Afterlife she approves of the way I still call on her lessons to help me see the way forward. Thank you my dear friend.